THE BEST OF DAYS

THE VIRTUES OF THE BLESSED TEN DAYS OF DHŪ AL-ḤIJJAH,
THE DAY OF 'ARAFAH, THE 'ĪD OF SACRIFICE,
AND THE DAYS OF AL-TASHRĪQ

from the
LAṬĀ'IF AL-MA'ĀRIF

of
IBN RAJAB AL-ḤANBALĪ

Translated by
MOHAMMED AHMED

Published By

White Fountain Publishing
Leicester, England

www.whitefountain.co.uk

admin@whitefountain.co.uk

The Best of Days
[Selections from the '*Laṭa'if al-Ma'ārif*' of Ibn Rajab al-Ḥanbalī]
Mohammed Ahmed

ISBN   978-1-7399907-3-2

Typesetting &   *MA, White Fountain Publishing*
Book Design

Cover Design   *MA, White Fountain Publishing*

لَا إِلٰهَ إِلَّا اللهُ وَحْدَهُ
لَا شَرِيكَ لَهُ
لَهُ الْمُلْكُ وَلَهُ الْحَمْدُ
وَهُوَ عَلَى كُلِّ شَيْءٍ قَدِيرٌ.

THE BEST REMEMBRANCE
FOR THE DAY OF ʿARAFAH

In the name of Allah, Most Gracious, Most Merciful.

All praise be to Allah, Lord of the Worlds.

Salutations, peace and blessings be upon His Messenger

Our Master Muḥammad, Mercy to the Worlds.

Transliteration & Honorifics Key

ا	', a, ā	ض	ḍ
ب	b	ط	ṭ
ت	t	ظ	ẓ
ث	th	ع	', ʿā, ʿī, ʿū
ج	j	غ	gh
ح	ḥ	ف	f
خ	kh	ق	q
د	d	ك	k
ذ	dh	ل	l
ر	r	م	m
ز	z	ن	n
س	s	و	w, ū, u
ش	sh	ه	h
ص	ṣ	ي	y, ī, i

Used following the mention of Prophet Muḥammad.
(*May the salutations and peace of Allah be upon him*)

Used after mention of an angel or a prophet.
(*May peace be upon him*)

Used after the mention of a noble Ṣaḥābī (Companion) of the Prophet.
(*May Allah be pleased with him*)

Used after mention of a scholar, saint, or pious person who has passed away.
(*May Allah shower His mercies upon him*)

Used after mention of two Companions.
(*May Allah be pleased with them both*)

Used after mention of two deceased pious persons.
(*May Allah shower His mercies upon them both*)

Used after mention of three or more Companions.
(*May Allah be pleased with them all*)

Used after mention of three or more deceased pious persons.
(*May Allah shower His mercies upon them all*)

Contents

Transliteration & Honorifics Key   5

Foreword by *Shaykh*   8

Preface   9

1. **Al-Majlis Al-Awwal:** *The Virtue of the Ten Days of Dhū al-Ḥijjah*   12

2. **Chapter One:** The Virtue of Actions Performed During These Days   13
The Superiority of Deeds in these Ten Days   13
The Increased Multiplication of Rewards and Merits for Deeds   14
Fasting in These Ten Days   16
Reviving the Ten Nights with Worship   18
The Dhikr of Allah in "The Known Days"   19
The Superiority of Pilgrimage or of Military Service   20
The Superiority of Good Deeds Performed during The Ten Days   23
The Fast of this Month & The Fasts of Ramaḍān   26

3. **Chapter Two:** The Superiority of The Ten Days of Dhū al-Ḥijjah Over Other Ten Days of Other Months   28
The Superiority of These Days In Relation to Friday   29
The Superiority of These Days   30
The Superiority of The Nights of Dhū al-Ḥijjah In Comparison to Laylat Al-Qadr   31
The Superiority of These Nights & Days In Comparison To Ramaḍān   32
The Superiority of Dhū Al-Ḥijjah In Comparison To The Other Sacred Months   33
The Virtues of These Ten Nights & Days   34
The Sacred Dawn   34
The Sacred Ten Nights   34
The Even & The Odd   35
The Ten within the 40 Days of Mūsā   36
From The Well-Known Months   37
The Days Of Dhikr   38

The Dhikr On The Sacrificial Animals   38
Dhikr & The Talbiyah   40
Dhikr & The Hajj   42
The Days of Dhū Al-Ḥijjah & The Non-Pilgrim   44
The Non-Pilgrim Offering The Sacrifice   44
The Non-Pilgrim's Du'ā & Dhikr   45
Advice For The Non-Pilgrim In These Blessed Days   47

4. Al-Majlis Al-Thānī: *The Virtue of the Day of 'Arafah & The Festival of Sacrifice*   52
Every Friday Is A Weekly 'Īd   54
Some Virtues of Jumu'ah (Friday)   55
The 'Īd Al-Fitr   56
The 'Īd Al-Aḍhā & The Day of 'Arafah   57
The Perfection Of Islam Revealed On The Day of 'Arafah   63
The Completion Of Allah's Favour Revealed On The Day of 'Arafah   64
Some Virtues of The Day Of 'Arafah   65
A Day Of Despondency & Humiliation For Satan   72
Attaining Forgiveness & Deliverance From Hellfire On The Day of 'Arafah   74
The Fast of The Day Of 'Arafah   74
The Best Dhikr For The Day Of 'Arafah   75
Freedom & Salvation   77
A Non-Pilgrim In The Season Of Hajj   84

5. Al-Majlis Al-Thālith: *The Days of Tashrīq*   88
The Appointed Days Of Festivity & Dhikr   88
The Appointed Days in Ḥajj   90
Dhikr Of Allah in The Appointed Days   92
A Recommended Sunnah Du'ā   94
A Time For Du'ā   95
Concluding All Rites With Dhikr   95
A Festivity Of Offering Thanks & Gratitude To Almighty Allah   97
Wisdoms Of Slaughtering The Sacrificial Animal   98
'Īd As Hospitality From Almighty Allah   100
The Rites: A Parable Of The Believer's Condition   102
Righteous Fasting   102
Paradise: The Hospitality of Almighty Allah   103
Our Festivals: Answering The Call Of Allah   105
Staying Away From Disobedience: The Ultimate Festival   106

Preface

Praise be to Allah, the Lord of the Worlds, and peace and blessings be upon the Seal of the Prophets, the Leader of both worlds, *Sayyidinā* Muḥammad ﷺ, and his family and Companions.

Most Muslims around the world are well-acquainted with the holy month of *Ramaḍān*, a time of fasting, prayer, and reflection. This blessed month holds a special place in the hearts of the *Ummah*, drawing widespread attention and devotion.

However, beyond *Ramaḍān*, there are other significant periods in the Islamic calendar that are equally deserving of our attention and reverence.

Among these are the first ten days of *Dhū al-Ḥijjah*, a time filled with immense blessings and opportunities for spiritual growth.

The ten days of *Dhū al-Ḥijjah* are considered the best days of the year, as attested by the teachings and traditions of the Prophet Muḥammad ﷺ.

These days encompass profound moments such as the Day of 'Arafah, the Festival of Sacrifice ('*Īd al-Aḍḥā*), and the days of *Tashrīq*.

For those who are not on the pilgrimage to the blessed lands of Makkah al-Mukarramah, these days still offer a chance to attain closeness to Allah through increased worship, supplication, and *dhikr*.

Classically, the pious and the scholars (*'ulamā'*) maintained a practice of paying significant attention to these blessed days. They increased their worship, fasting, and *dhikr* (remembrance of Almighty Allah) during this period.

Throughout my time in the company and service of my respected Honourable Late *Shaykh*, Shaykh Yūsuf Motālā [*May Allah fill his grave with Divine light*], I witnessed firsthand how these days were observed with great reverence and dedication.

At the Darul 'Uloom in Bury, Greater Manchester, Shaykh Yūsuf ؓ would arrange and organise gatherings in the Masjid of Darul 'Uloom, specifically for increased voluntary worship.

He himself would fast these days, breaking his fast with a small bottle of water that he kept in his pocket. After the *Maghrib Ṣalāh*, he would engage in prolonged units of *nafl* prayers, sometimes extending right until just before *'Ishā' Ṣalāh*.

The attendees, students, and disciples would be engaged in individual worship, with many reciting the Noble Qur'ān, performing *dhikr*, and offering *nafl Ṣalāh*.

In his latter years, Shaykh Yūsuf ؓ would organise for disciples and visitors to attend Darul 'Uloom and partake in these blessed gatherings, encouraging everyone to appreciate and strive extra hard during these best days of the year.

THIS BOOK:

In this book, which I have titled "The Best of Days," I have translated selected chapters from the esteemed work *'Laṭā'if al-Ma'ārif'* by the renowned scholar Imām Ibn Rajab Al-Ḥanbalī ؓ.

This book provides an in-depth exploration of the virtues and significance of these blessed days.

It is a treasure trove of knowledge that sheds light on the merits of the ten days of Dhū al-Ḥijjah, the importance of the Day of 'Arafah, the profound wisdoms and meanings behind the *ʿĪd al-Aḍḥā*, and the practices to be observed during these ten days, and what follows from the days of *Tashrīq*.

As part of this translation, I have added titles and sub-headings to various topics, themes, and discussions presented in the original work. These additions are designed to help readers navigate the text more easily, allowing for a more structured and accessible reading experience.

This translation aims to bring this valuable knowledge to the English-speaking Muslim community. It serves as a guide for families, Muslim homes, and Islamic circles to better understand and appreciate these sacred days.

The eloquence and depth of Ibn Rajab Al-Ḥanbalī's discussions offer a rich source of knowledge that can be incorporated into courses, lectures, and personal study.

By delving into this book, readers will discover the great virtues that lie within these ten days and how they stand as the best days of the year.

It is my hope that this work will inspire a greater awareness and devotion towards these blessed days, enriching our spiritual lives and drawing us closer to our Creator.

As we approach the blessed month of Dhū al-Ḥijjah, we beseech that Almighty Allah accept our efforts, forgive our shortcomings, and grant us the ability to fully benefit from these precious days.

May eternal and everlasting blessings be upon our Master Muḥammad ﷺ, his family, his Companions, and all those who follow him from his blessed nation. *Āmīn.*

Mohammed bin Khalid Ahmed
White Fountain Publishing   31 May 2024
Leicester, UK   23 Dhū al-Qaʿdah 1445 A.H.

Imām Ibn Rajab al-Ḥanbalī writes:

FUNCTIONS OF THE MONTH OF DHŪ AL-ḤIJJAH

This chapter includes the following sections:

AL-MAJLIS AL-AWWAL: THE VIRTUE OF THE TEN DAYS OF DHŪ AL-ḤIJJAH

Al-Bukhārī narrated from the *ḥadīth* of Ibn ʿAbbās ﷺ that the Prophet ﷺ said: "*There are no days in which righteous deeds are more beloved to Allah than these days - meaning the ten days (of Dhū al-Ḥijjah)."* They asked:

"O Messenger of Allah, not even military service in the way of Allah?" He ﷺ said: "*Not even military service in the way of Allah, except for a man who goes out with himself and his wealth and returns with nothing."* [1]

The discussion on the virtue of the ten days of Dhū al-Ḥijjah is divided into two aspects:

(1) The virtue of actions performed during these days, as indicated by this *ḥadīth*, and

(2) The intrinsic virtue of these days themselves.

---

[1] Reported by Bukhārī (969), Abū Dawūd (2438), Tirmidhī (757), and Ibn Mājah (1727).

Chapter One

THE VIRTUE OF ACTIONS
PERFORMED DURING THESE DAYS

The *ḥadīth* indicates that actions performed during these days are more beloved to Allah than actions performed during any other days of the year, without exception. If they are more beloved to Allah, then they are superior in His sight.

This *ḥadīth* has also been narrated with the wording: "*There are no days in which deeds are better than the days of the ten.*"

There is also a narration with uncertainty in its wording, between "*more beloved*" and "better."

THE SUPERIORITY OF DEEDS IN THESE TEN DAYS

If the deeds performed during the ten days are better and more beloved to Allah than deeds during any other days of the year, then deeds performed during these days, even if they are considered less significant, become better than more significant deeds performed at other times.

This is why they asked: "O Messenger of Allah, not even striving in the way of Allah?" He said: "*Not even striving,*" and then he excepted one type of military service, which is the best form of struggle. The Prophet ﷺ was asked: "Which struggle is the most superior?" He said:

13

"The one in which a man's horse is wounded and his blood is shed."[1] As such, the one who performs such a struggle may hold the highest rank before Allah.

The Prophet ﷺ heard a man praying, saying: "O Allah, give me the best of what You give Your righteous servants." He said to him: *"Then your horse will be wounded, and you will be martyred."*[2]. This specific form of military service may be better than deeds in the ten days.

As for the rest of the types of military service, deeds during the ten days of Dhū al-Ḥijjah are superior and more beloved to Almighty Allah than them, as well as all other deeds.

This indicates that less significant deeds in a virtuous time become equivalent to more significant deeds at other times, and even surpass them due to the multiplication of their rewards and merits.

THE INCREASED MULTIPLICATION OF REWARDS AND MERITS FOR DEEDS

It has been narrated in the *ḥadīth* of Ibn 'Abbās ﷺ with the addition: *"Deeds in these days are multiplied seven hundred times,"* though its chain of transmission is weak.

Various narrations mention the extent of this multiplication. Al-Tirmidhī and Ibn Mājah reported from the narration of Al-Nahhas ibn Qahm, from Qatādah, from Ibn al-Musayyib, from Abū Hurairah ﷺ, that the Prophet ﷺ said:

"There are no days more beloved to Allah for worship than the ten days of Dhū al-Ḥijjah. Fasting each day is equivalent to fasting a year, and praying each night is equivalent to praying on the Night of Decree."[3]

---

[1] Reported by Abū Dawūd (1449), and Nasā'ī (5/58) with similarity in meaning.
[2] Reported by Ḥākim (2/74), Ibn Ḥibbān (4639). Refer also to the '*Al-Tārikh al-Kabīr*' of Al-Bukhārī (1/222), '*Al-Tamhīd*' by Ibn 'Abd al-Barr (1/237), and the ' *'Ilal* ' of al-Dāraquṭnī. (4/342).
[3] Reported by Tirmidhī (758), Ibn Mājah (1728). Refer also to: "*Ilal al-Dāraquṭnī*' (9/199-203).

Thawīr ibn Abī Fākhitah, who is also weak, narrated from Mujāhid, from Ibn 'Umar ﷺ, that he said: "There is no day greater before Allah than Friday, except the ten days; for deeds in them are equivalent to deeds of a year."

Abū 'Amr al-Naysābūrī reported in his '*Kitāb al-Ḥikāyāt*' with his chain of transmission from Ḥumayd, who said: "I heard Ibn Sīrīn and Qatādah say that fasting each day of the ten is equivalent to fasting a year."

There are also [other] narrations suggesting even greater multiplications.

Hārūn ibn Mūsā al-Naḥwī narrated that he heard Al-Ḥasan reporting from Anas ibn Mālik ﷺ that it was said during the ten days: "Each day is equivalent to a thousand days, and the Day of 'Arafah is equivalent to ten thousand days."

Al-Ḥākim said: This is from the *musnads* (reports attributed directly to the Prophet ﷺ) whose chain of transmission is not mentioned.

There are also narrations with multiplication of deeds equivalent to being less than a year.

Ḥumayd ibn Zanjūyah reported that Yaḥyā ibn 'Abdillah al-Ḥarrāni narrated from Abū Bakr ibn Abī Maryam, from Rashīd ibn Sa'd, that the Prophet ﷺ said: "*Fasting each day of the ten days is equivalent to fasting a month.*"[1]

This is a *mursal* narration with a weak chain of transmission. 'Abdul Razzaq narrated in his book from Ja'far, from Hishām, from Al-Ḥasan, who said: "Fasting one day of the ten is equivalent to fasting two months."[2]

Al-Nahhas ibn Qahm was considered weak. Tirmidhī mentioned that Bukhārī reported the *ḥadīth* from Qatādah, from Sa'īd, as a *mursal* (unlinked) narration.

[1] Attributed in '*Kanz al-'Ummāl*' (12117) to Ibn Zanjūyah only.

[2] Reported by 'Abd al-Razzāq in his '*Muṣannaf*' (8126).

'Abd al-Karīm narrated from Mujāhid: "Deeds during the ten days are multiplied."

There are other *marfū'* (elevated to the Prophet ﷺ) narrations about the multiplication of deeds, but they are fabricated, so we have avoided them and similar fabrications about the virtues of the ten days, which are many.

The *ḥadīth* of Ibn Abbas ﷺ indicates the multiplication of all righteous deeds during the ten days without exception.

FASTING IN THESE TEN DAYS

There are specific narrations about fasting during these days, praying at night, and frequent remembrance, which are worth mentioning, though not all are authentic.

The *ḥadīth* of Abū Hurayrah ﷺ and the *mursal* narration of Rashīd ibn Sa'd, and what has been reported from Al-Ḥasan, Ibn Sīrīn, and Qatādah about fasting have been mentioned.

In '*Al-Musnad*' and '*Al-Sunan*' from Ḥafṣah ﷺ that the Prophet ﷺ "would not abandon fasting on 'Āshūrā', the ten days, and three days of each month."[1] There is a disagreement in its chain of transmission.

It is narrated from some of the wives of the Prophet ﷺ "that the Prophet ﷺ would not abandon fasting the nine days of Dhū al-Ḥijjah."[2]

Among those who used to fast the ten days was 'Abdullāh ibn Umar ﷺ. The virtue of fasting has been mentioned by Al-Ḥasan, Ibn Sīrīn, and Qatādah, and it is the opinion of most scholars, or many of them.

---

[1] Reported by Aḥmad (6/287), Nasā'ī (4/220). Zayla'ī said in 'Naṣb al-Rāyah': weak.
[2] Reported by Abū Dawūd (2437).

In 'Ṣaḥīḥ Muslim' from 'Ā'ishah ﷺ may Allah be pleased with her, she said: "I never saw the Messenger of Allah ﷺ fasting the ten days." In another narration: "during the ten days."[1]

Imām Aḥmad had different responses to this *ḥadīth*; once he responded that the contrary has been narrated, and mentioned the *ḥadīth* of Ḥafṣah ﷺ, hinting that there is a difference in the chain of transmission of 'Ā'ishah's *ḥadīth*; Al-A'mash narrated it, and Manṣūr narrated it from Ibrāhīm as a *mursal* narration.

Other scholars responded similarly, stating that if there is a contradiction between 'Ā'ishah ﷺ and Ḥafṣah ﷺ regarding negation and affirmation, the statement of the affirming one is taken, because they have knowledge that was hidden from the one negating.

Another time, Aḥmad responded that 'Ā'ishah ﷺ meant that he did not fast the entire ten days completely, meaning that Ḥafṣah ﷺ meant that he would fast most of them; hence, it is recommended to fast some and break the fast on others.

This reconciliation is valid for the narration: "I never saw him fasting the ten days."

As for the narration: "I never saw him fasting during the ten days," this reconciliation is more challenging or impossible.

Ibn Sīrīn disliked saying: "He fasted the ten days," because it gives the impression that the fasting includes *Yawm al-Naḥr* (the Day of Sacrifice). Instead, it should be said: "He fasted the nine days," but when fasting is mentioned in the context of the ten days, it means fasting the days that are permissible to fast from them.

It has been previously mentioned that the Prophet ﷺ used to fast the ten days.

---

[1] Reported by Muslim (1176), Aḥmad (190, 124), Abū Dawūd (2439), Tirmidhī (756), Ibn Khuzaymah (2103), and Ibn Mājah (1729).

If someone vowed to fast the ten days, it should be understood as fasting the nine days, so fasting on the ʿĪd al-Aḍḥā (*Yawm al-Naḥr*) would not require making up or expiation, as it is generally understood to mean fasting the nine days.

There may be a difference of opinion regarding the obligation of making up and expiation. Imām Aḥmad said that if someone vowed to fast the month of Shawwāl but broke the fast on the Day of ʿĪd and then fasted the rest, he would have to make up one day and give expiation.

The judge, Qāḍī Abū Yaʿlā said: This is if he intended to fast the entire month; but if he left it unspecified, he would not be obligated to anything because the Day of ʿĪd is legally excluded.

This is one of the principles of jurisprudence, whether general terms are restricted by legal exceptions or not, and there is a well-known disagreement on this issue.

REVIVING THE TEN NIGHTS WITH WORSHIP

As for praying during the nights of the ten days, it is recommended, and this has been previously mentioned.

There are specific narrations about reviving the two nights of ʿĪd [by staying awake with worship during them] which are not authentic, but there are narrations about answered prayers on these nights, and it is recommended by Imām Shāfiʿī and other scholars.

Saʿīd ibn Jubayr, who narrated this *ḥadīth* from Ibn ʿAbbas ﷺ, would exert himself greatly during the ten days, to the extent that he could hardly bear it.

It was reported that he said: "Do not extinguish your lamps during the nights of the ten days, as worship is beloved to Him (i.e., Allah)."

THE DHIKR OF ALLAH IN "THE KNOWN DAYS"

As for the recommendation to increase in remembrance during these days, it is indicated by the words of Almighty Allah:

﴿ وَيَذْكُرُوا اسْمَ اللَّهِ فِي أَيَّامٍ مَّعْلُومَاتٍ ﴾

And mention the name of Allah in the known days [Al-Ḥajj : 28]

The "known days" are the ten days according to the majority of scholars. This will be further explained later, *in-shā'-Allāh*.

In the '*Musnad*' of Imām Aḥmad, it is narrated from Ibn 'Umar ﷺ, that the Prophet ﷺ said:

« مَا مِن أَيَّامٍ أَعْظَمَ [عِنْدَ الله] وَلَا أَحَبَّ إِلَيْهِ العَمَلَ فِيهِنَّ مِن هَذِهِ الأَيَّامِ العَشْرِ ،
فَأَكْثِرُوا فِيهِنَّ مِنَ التَّهْلِيلِ وَالتَّكْبِيرِ وَالتَّحْمِيدِ »

There are no days greater [before Allah] and more beloved to Him for good deeds than these ten days, so increase in them the tahlīl, takbīr, and taḥmīd. [1]

The essence of the *ḥadīth* is found in the two '*Ṣaḥīḥ*'s from the *ḥadīth* of Ibn 'Abbās ﷺ as previously mentioned.

---

[1] Reported by Aḥmad (5446, 2/75)

Tahlīl: Saying لَا إِلَهَ إِلَّا الله

Takbīr: Saying اللهُ أَكْبَرُ

Taḥmīd: Saying الحَمْدُ لله

THE SUPERIORITY OF PILGRIMAGE
OR OF MILITARY SERVICE

If it is said: If deeds performed during the ten days are better than deeds performed at other times, even if those deeds are inherently better than those performed during the ten days due to the virtue of the ten days themselves, then the less significant deeds performed during them become significant to the extent that they surpass military service, which is one of the best deeds, as indicated by numerous texts. This is the opinion of Imām Aḥmad and other scholars.

Thus, Ḥajj should be better than military service because Ḥajj is specific to the ten days and is among the best deeds performed during these days, or the best deed performed during them.

So how is it that military service may be considered better than Ḥajj? It is established in the two 'Ṣaḥīḥ's from Abū Hurayrah ﷺ that a man said: "O Messenger of Allah, which deed is best?" He said:

« إِيَمَانٌ بِاللهِ وَرَسُولِهِ »

Faith in Allah and His Messenger.

He said: "Then what?" He ﷺ said:

« جِهَادٌ فِي سَبِيلِ اللهِ »

Military service in the way of Allah.

He said: "Then what?" He said:

« حَجٌّ مَبْرُورٌ »

A mabrūr (complete and accepted righteous) Ḥajj. [1]

---

[1] Reported by Bukhārī (26), Muslim (83), Nasā'ī (5/113), and Tirmidhī (1658).

It is said that voluntary military service is better than voluntary Ḥajj according to the majority of scholars, and this was explicitly stated by Imām Aḥmad.

This is also narrated from ‘Abdullāh ibn ‘Amr ibn al-‘Āṣ ﷺ.

There are *marfū‘* narrations about this, but their chains of transmission are questionable. The *ḥadīth* of Abū Hurayrah ﷺ is explicit in this regard. There are two ways to reconcile it with the *ḥadīth* of Ibn ‘Abbās ﷺ.

Firstly, the *ḥadīth* of Ibn ‘Abbās ﷺ explicitly states that the struggle of one who does not return with anything of himself, or his wealth, is superior to deeds during the ten days.

Therefore, it can be said that Ḥajj is better than military service, except for the struggle of one who does not return with anything of himself or his wealth, which would be the meaning intended in the *ḥadīth* of Abū Hurayrah ﷺ, thus reconciling the two *ḥadīths*.

Secondly, and this is more apparent, is that a less significant deed may be accompanied by something that makes it superior to a deed that is inherently better, as previously mentioned.

Therefore, Ḥajj may be accompanied by something that makes it better than military service, or it may lack that, making military service better at that time.

If Ḥajj is obligatory, it is better than voluntary military service, because individual obligations are better than collective obligations according to the majority of scholars.

This has been specifically narrated regarding Ḥajj and military service from ‘Abdullāh ibn ‘Amr ibn al-‘Āṣ ﷺ and has been elevated [in ascription to the Prophet ﷺ] from multiple sources, though their chains are weak.

This is supported by what the Prophet ﷺ narrated from his Lord, the Almighty, who said:

« مَا تَقَرَّبَ إِلَيَّ عَبْدِي بِمِثْلِ أَدَاءِ مَا افْتَرَضْتُ عَلَيْهِ »

*My servant does not draw near to Me with anything
more beloved to Me than what I have obligated upon him.*[1]

as part of the ḥadīth of Abū Hurayrah, the beginning of which is:

« مَنْ عَادَى لِي وَلِيًّا فَقَدْ آذَنْتُهُ بِالحَرْبِ ... »

*Whoever shows enmity to a walī (friend) of Mine,
I have declared war against him...*

If the pilgrim is not one of those obligated to participate in military service, then his Ḥajj is better than his military service, like in the case of a woman.

It is narrated in 'Ṣaḥīḥ Al-Bukhārī' from 'Ā'ishah ﷺ that she said:

يا رسول الله ! نرى الجهاد أفضل العمل ، أفلا نجاهد ؟

*O Messenger of Allah, we see military service as the best deed,
should we not engage in the struggle?*

He ﷺ said:

« أَفْضَلُ الجِهَادِ حَجٌّ مَبْرُورٌ »

The best jihād is a mabrūr (complete and accepted righteous) Ḥajj.[2]

In another narration:

« جِهَادُكُنَّ الحَجُّ »

Your jihād is the Ḥajj.

In another narration:

---

[1] Reported by Bukhārī (6502).
[2] Reported by Bukhārī (1520), and Nasā'ī (5/114-115).

« نَعَم ، الْجِهَاد الْحَجّ »

Yes, the (best) jihād is the Ḥajj.

Similarly, if the entire ten days are consumed by the acts of Ḥajj, performed in the best manner by fulfilling obligations and avoiding prohibitions, along with acts of kindness towards people like spreading peace and feeding food, and also includes frequent *dhikr* (remembrance) of Almighty Allah, and the "al-'Ajj" (raising the voice with the *talbiyah*) and "al-Thajj" (sacrificing the animals), then such a Ḥajj may be better than military service.

If the acts of Ḥajj take up only a small part of the ten days and are not performed in the best manner, then military service could be better than it.

It has been narrated from 'Umar, Ibn 'Umar, Abū Mūsā Al-Ash'arī ﷺ, and also from Mujāhid, indicating the preference of Ḥajj over military service and other deeds, which should be understood as referring to a righteous Ḥajj that is performed perfectly and takes up the entire ten days. And Allah knows best.

THE SUPERIORITY OF GOOD DEEDS PERFORMED DURING THE TEN DAYS

If it is said: Does the statement of the Prophet ﷺ:

« مَا مِن أَيَّامٍ العَمَل الصَّالِح فِيهَا أَحَبّ إِلَى الله مِن هَذِهِ الأَيَّامِ »

*"There are no days in which righteous deeds are
more beloved to Allah than these days;"*

imply that every righteous deed performed during the ten days is preferred over all deeds performed at other times, even if their duration is longer or not?

It is said: The apparent meaning - and Allah knows best - is that deeds performed during these ten days are better than deeds performed during any other ten days, so every righteous deed performed during these ten days is better than a deed performed during any other ten days, from any month.

This preference applies to deeds performed on each day of the ten over deeds performed on any other day of the year.

It has been said: Righteous deeds are preferred over military service during these days if they encompass the entire ten days, making them better than military service of the same duration outside of the ten days. If the deeds occupy only some of the ten days, they are better than military service of the same duration outside of the ten days.

This is supported by the fact that the Prophet ﷺ equated continuous deeds such as fasting and praying [within these ten days] with military service at any time.

If such continuous deeds are performed during the ten days, they are better than military service of the same duration, due to the virtue and honour of the ten days.

In the two 'Ṣaḥīḥ's, it is narrated that Abū Hurayrah ﷺ said: A man came to the Messenger of Allah ﷺ and said, "Guide me to a deed equivalent to military service." He ﷺ said, "*I do not find one.*" He said, "When the one striving in military service goes out, can you enter your place of prayer and stand in prayer without tiring and fast without breaking your fast?" He said, "Who can do that?" [1]

The wording is from Bukhārī, and Muslim has a similar meaning with the addition of:

---

[1] Reported by Bukhārī (2785), Muslim (1878), and Nasā'ī (6/19).

Then he said: "*The example of the one who struggles in the way of Allah is like the one who fasts and prays continually, who does not become weary of prayer or fasting until the one striving in the way of Allah returns.*"

And in Bukhārī: "*The example of the one who strives in the way of Allah - and Allah knows best who struggles in His way - is like the one who fasts and prays continuously.*"

And in Nasā'ī: "*Like the one who fasts, prays, humbles himself, and bows and prostrates.*" [1]

Also, it indicates that the intended meaning is the preference of deeds during these days over military service of the same duration, specifically in the *ḥadīth* from the 'Ṣaḥīḥ' of Ibn Ḥibbān, from Jābir ﷺ, who narrates from the Prophet ﷺ, who said:

$$\text{« مَا مِن أَيَّامٍ أَفْضَلُ عِنْدَ الله مِن أَيَّامِ عَشْرِ ذِي الحِجَّة »}$$

There are no days better in the sight of Allah
than the days of the ten days of Dhū al-Ḥijjah.

A man asked: "O Messenger of Allah, are they better or equivalent to the same number of days in military service in the way of Allah?" He said:

$$\text{« هُوَ أَفْضَلُ مِن عِدَّتِهِنَّ جِهَادًا في سَبِيلِ الله »}$$

They are better than the same number of days
in military service in the way of Allah. [2]

So, it could be that the preference is given to the righteous deeds during the ten days over military service of the same duration, not military service in general.

---

[1] Reported by Nasā'ī (6/18).
[2] Reported by Ibn Ḥibbān (3853).

THE FAST OF THIS MONTH & THE FASTS OF RAMADĀN

As for what has been previously mentioned that each day is equivalent to a year or two months or a thousand days, these are all from the weak *ḥadīths* regarding virtues.

Moreover, most of these narrations refer to fasting, which has a specific virtue in terms of multiplication of reward, as fasting is for Allah, and He rewards it.

If it is said that this does not only apply to fasting but includes all deeds, it means that every deed performed during the ten days is better than the same deed performed during other days of the year, and this includes the preference of military service during the ten days over military service during other times of the year.

If it is said: This would imply that fasting during these ten days is better than fasting during the ten days of *Ramaḍān*, and praying at night during these days is better than praying at night during *Ramaḍān*.

It is said: As for fasting during *Ramaḍān*, it is undoubtedly better than fasting during these ten days because obligatory fasting is better than voluntary fasting without doubt.

Thus, the intended meaning is that what is done in the ten days of obligatory acts is better than what is done in other ten days of obligatory acts, so obligatory prayers during these ten days are multiplied over obligatory prayers during the ten days of *Ramaḍān*.

Similarly, voluntary acts done during these ten days are better than voluntary acts done during other times.

There was a difference of opinion between 'Umar and 'Alī ﷺ regarding making up missed *Ramaḍān* fasts during the ten days of *Dhū al-Ḥijjah.*

'Umar preferred it due to the virtue of these days, making up *Ramaḍān* fasts during these days better than other times, indicating the multiplication of obligatory acts over voluntary acts during these days.

'Alī ﷺ forbade it. There are two narrations from Aḥmad on this matter.

'Alī's ﷺ opinion was explained that making up fasts during these days would miss the virtue of fasting voluntarily, and Imām Aḥmad and others explained it similarly.

It has been said: It also attains the virtue of voluntary fasting, which is the opinion of those who say that if one vows to fast for a month and then fasts during *Ramaḍān*, it fulfils his vow, and this opinion has merit, and it has been explained in other ways as well.

As for praying during the nights and preferring it over the ten nights of *Ramaḍān*, this will be discussed, *in-shā-Allāh*.

Chapter Two

THE SUPERIORITY OF THE TEN DAYS OF DHŪ AL-ḤIJJAH
OVER OTHER TEN DAYS OF OTHER MONTHS

It has been previously mentioned in the *ḥadīth* narrated by Ibn ʿUmar ﷺ, that the Prophet ﷺ said: "There are no days greater in the sight of Allah and more beloved to Him for deeds than these ten days."

In 'Ṣaḥīḥ Ibn Ḥibbān', it is narrated from Jābir ﷺ, that the Prophet ﷺ said:

« مَا مِن أَيَّامٍ أَفْضَلُ عِنْدَ الله مِن أَيَّامِ عَشْرِ ذِي الحِجَّة »

There are no days better in the sight of Allah
than the days of the ten days of Dhū al-Ḥijjah;

as previously mentioned.

We also narrated it from another source with the addition:

« وَلَا لَيَالِيَ أَفْضَلُ مِنْ لَيَالِيهِنَّ »

Nor are there nights better than their nights.

It was said: "O Messenger of Allah, are they better than the same number of days in military service in the way of Allah?" He said:

« هُنَّ أَفْضَلُ مِن عِدَّتِهِنَّ جِهَادًا فِي سَبِيلِ الله ، إِلَّا مَنْ عَفَّرَ وَجْهَهُ تَعْفِيرًا .
وَمَا مِن يَوْمٍ أَفْضَلُ مِنْ يَوْمِ عَرَفَة ... »

They are better than the same number of days in military service in the way of Allah, except for one who dirties his face with dust. And there is no day better than the Day of ʿArafah.

Ḥāfiẓ Abū Mūsā Al-Madani reported it from Abū Nuʿaym Al-Ḥāfiẓ with the same chain of transmission used by Ibn Ḥibbān.

Bazzār and others also narrated from Jābir ﷺ that the Prophet ﷺ said:

« أَفْضَلُ أَيَّامِ الدُّنْيَا أَيَّامُ العَشرِ . »

The best days in the world are the ten days (of Dhū al-Ḥijjah)

They asked: "O Messenger of Allah, not even the same number of days in the way of Allah?" He said:

« وَلَا مِثْلُهُنَّ فِي سَبِيلِ اللهِ ، إِلَّا مَن عَفَّرَ وَجْهَهُ بِالتُّرَابِ »

Not even the same number of days in the way of Allah,
except for one who dirties his face with dust. [1]

It was also narrated as *mursal* (disconnected), and it is said that this is more authentic.

THE SUPERIORITY OF THESE DAYS IN RELATION TO FRIDAY

It has been previously mentioned in what was narrated from Ibn ʿUmar ﷺ, who said: "There is no day greater in the sight of Allah than Friday, except for the ten days."

This indicates that the ten days are better than Friday, which is the best of days.

---

[1] Reported by Bazzār (1128 – ʿ*Kashf*ʾ), and Shajarī in ʿ*Al-Amālī*ʾ (2/62).

THE SUPERIORITY OF THESE DAYS

Suhail ibn Abī Ṣāliḥ narrated from his father, from Ka'b, who said: "Allah chose the time, and the most beloved time to Allah is the sacred month, and the most beloved of the sacred months to Allah is Dhū al-Ḥijjah, and the most beloved part of Dhū al-Ḥijjah to Allah is its first ten days."

Some narrated this from Suhail, from his father, from Abū Hurayrah ﷺ, and elevated it by ascribing it to the Prophet ﷺ; but this is not authentic.

Masrūq said regarding Allah's words: [٢ : الفجر] ﴿ وَلَيَالٍ عَشْرٍ ﴾ that "These are the best days of the year."

'Abd al-Razzāq and others narrated it. [1]

Also, within these ten days is included the Day of 'Arafah, which is reported to be the best day of the world - as in the ḥadīth of Jabir that we mentioned - and it also includes:

« يَوْم النَّحْرِ »

Yawm al-Naḥr (The Day of Sacrifice).

In the ḥadīth of 'Abdullāh ibn Qurṭ, the Prophet ﷺ said:

« أَعْظَمُ الأَيَّامِ عِنْدَ الله يَوْمُ النَّحْرِ ، ثُمَّ يَوْمُ القَرِّ »

The greatest days in the sight of Allah are
the Day of Sacrifice and then the Day of Rest.

This was reported by Imām Aḥmad , Abū Dāwūd, and others. [2]

All of this indicates that the ten days of Dhū al-Ḥijjah are better than any other days without exception; this applies to its days.

---

[1] Reported by 'Abd al-Razzāq in his '*Muṣannaf*' (8120).
[2] Reported by Aḥmad (4/350), Abū Dawūd (1765), Ḥākim (4/221), and Ibn Khuzaymah (2917, 2866).

THE SUPERIORITY OF THE NIGHTS OF DHŪ AL-ḤIJJAH IN COMPARISON TO LAYLAT AL-QADR

As for its nights, some later scholars have claimed that the nights of the ten days of *Ramaḍān* are better than its nights because they include *Laylat al-Qadr*, but this is far-fetched.

If the *ḥadīth* of Abū Hurayrah ﷺ:

» قِيَامُ كُلِّ لَيْلَةٍ مِنْهَا بِقِيَام لَيْلَةِ القَدْر «

Each night of them is equivalent to Laylat al-Qadr. [1]

were authentic, it would be explicit in preferring its nights over the nights of the ten days of *Ramaḍān*, for the ten days of *Ramaḍān* are preferred by one night, while all these nights would be equivalent in standing in prayer according to this *ḥadīth*.

However, the *ḥadīth* of Jabir ﷺ reported by Abū Mūsā explicitly favours its nights just as its days are favoured.

When days are mentioned, nights are included as well, and similarly, when nights are mentioned, days are included.

Allah swore by its nights, saying:

﴿ وَالْفَجْرِ ۝ وَلَيَالٍ عَشْرٍ ﴾

By the dawn, and by the ten nights.
[Al-Fajr: 1-2]

This indicates the virtue of its nights as well, but it has not been established that its nights or any part of them are equivalent to *Laylat al-Qadr*.

Some groups among our scholars claimed that the night of Friday is better than *Laylat al-Qadr*, but this is not authentically attributed to Aḥmad.

---

[1] Reported by Tirmidhī (758), and Ibn Mājah (1728) and previously mentioned the weakening of the author. Refer to the ''Ilal' of Dāraquṭnī (9/199).

According to these scholars, it would not be far-fetched to prefer the nights of these ten days over Laylat al-Qadr.

THE SUPERIORITY OF THESE NIGHTS & DAYS IN COMPARISON TO RAMAḌĀN

The correct view, as stated by some prominent later scholars, is to say that the entirety of these ten days is better than the entirety of the ten days of *Ramaḍān*, even though there is a night in the ten days of *Ramaḍān* that is not surpassed by any other night; and Allah knows best.

What was previously mentioned from Ka'b indicates that the month of Dhū al-Ḥijjah is the best of the four sacred months.

This was also stated by Sa'īd ibn Jubayr, who narrated this *ḥadīth* from Ibn 'Abbās :

« مَا مِنَ الشُّهُورِ شَهْرٌ أَعْظَمُ حُرْمَةً مِن ذِي الْحِجَّةِ »

There is no month greater in sanctity than Dhū al-Ḥijjah.

In '*Musnad al-Bazzār*', it is narrated from Abū Sa'īd Al-Khudrī , from the Prophet , who said:

« سَيِّدُ الشُّهُورِ رَمَضَان ، وَأَعْظَمُهَا حُرْمَةً ذُو الْحِجَّة »

The best month is Ramaḍān, and the greatest in sanctity is Dhū al-Ḥijjah. [1]

The chain of transmission is weak.

---

[1] Reported by Bazzār (960 – '*Kashf*'). In its chain of transmission is Yazīd ibn 'Abd al-Malik Al-Nawfalī, and Bazzār said: "There is some weakness in him."

THE SUPERIORITY OF DHŪ AL-ḤIJJAH IN COMPARISON TO THE OTHER SACRED MONTHS

In '*Musnad al-Imām Aḥmad*', it is also narrated from Abū Saʿīd Al-Khudrī ﷺ, that the Prophet ﷺ said in his sermon on the Day of *Naḥr* (Sacrifice) during the Farewell Pilgrimage:

« أَلَا إِنَّ أَحْرَمَ الأَيَّامِ يَوْمُكُم هَذَا ، أَلَا وَإِنَّ أَحْرَمَ الشُّهُورِ شَهْرُكُم هَذَا ،

أَلَا وَإِنَّ أَحْرَمَ البِلَادِ بَلَدُكُم هَذَا »

*Indeed, the most sacred day is your day today, the most sacred month
is your month, and the most sacred place is your place.* [1]

This was also narrated from Jābir, Wābiṣah ibn Maʿbad, Nabīṭ ibn Sharīṭ, and others, from the Prophet ﷺ.

All of this indicates that the month of Dhū al-Ḥijjah is the best of the sacred months, being the most sanctified among them.

It was also narrated from Al-Ḥasan that the best of them is *Muḥarram*, which we will mention when discussing the month of *Muḥarram*, *in-shā'-Allāh*.

As for those who said that the best of them is *Rajab*, their opinion is rejected.

---

[1] Reported by Aḥmad (3/80), Ibn Mājah (3931). The essence of the *ḥadīth* is in the two 'Ṣaḥīḥ's from the *ḥadīth* of Abū Bakrah ﷺ.

THE VIRTUES OF THESE TEN NIGHTS & DAYS

The ten days of Dhū al-Ḥijjah have other virtues in addition to those mentioned earlier.

❖ Among its virtues is that **Allah the Almighty swore by it in general and by specific parts of it.**

Allah said:

﴿ وَالْفَجْرِ ① وَلَيَالٍ عَشْرٍ ﴾

By the dawn, and by the ten nights.
[Al-Fajr: 1-2]

THE SACRED DAWN

As for "*the dawn,*" it is said that it refers to the general time of dawn. It is also said that it refers to the rising of the dawn, or the dawn prayer, or the entire day; there is a difference of opinion among the interpreters.

It is also said that it refers to a specific dawn. Then it is said that it refers to the dawn of the first day of the ten days of Dhū al-Ḥijjah.

It is also said that it refers to the dawn of the last day of it, which is the Day of *Naḥr*. According to all these opinions, the ten days include the dawn that Allah swore by.

THE SACRED TEN NIGHTS

As for "*the ten nights,*" they are the ten days of Dhū al-Ḥijjah; this is the correct view held by the majority of the interpreters from the predecessors and others, and it is the correct opinion from Ibn 'Abbās; it is narrated from him through multiple chains.

The narration from him that "it is the ten days of *Ramaḍān*" has a weak chain of transmission.

THE EVEN & THE ODD

There is a *marfū' ḥadīth* reported by Aḥmad and Nasā'ī, from the narration of Zayd ibn Al-Ḥabbāb, who said: 'Ayyāsh ibn 'Aqabah narrated to us, who said: Khayr ibn Na'īm narrated to us, from Abū Al-Zubayr, from Jābir, from the Prophet ﷺ who said:

« العَشْرُ عَشْرُ الأضحى ، وَالوَتْرُ يَوْمُ عَرَفَة ، وَالشَّفْعُ يَوْمُ النَّحْر »

The "'ashr" (ten) are the ten days of the sacrifice, the "watr" (odd) is the
Day of 'Arafah, and the "Shaf" (even) is the Day of Naḥr (Sacrifice). [1]

It is a good chain of narration.

Similarly, Ibn 'Abbās ﷺ interpreted ﴿ الشَّفْع ﴾ *"the even"* and ﴿ الوَتْرِ ﴾ *"the odd"* in a narration from 'Ikrimah and others.

'Ikrimah, Al-Ḍaḥḥāk, and several others also interpreted them this way.

Many interpretations have been given for *"the even"* and *"the odd,"* but most revolve around the idea that the ten days or part of them include *"the even"* and *"the odd,"* or one of them.

For instance, some said: It refers to the prayer, some of which are even and some are odd.[2]

---

[1] Reported by Aḥmad (3/327), Bazzār (2286 – '*Kashf*'), and Ibn Jarīr in his '*Tafsīr*' (169/30) with only the first part.

Ḥāfiẓ Ibn Kathīr commented in his '*Tafsīr*' (8/413): This chain of narration has reliable narrators, but I find the text in its elevation in ascription [to the Prophet ﷺ] to be unusual, and Allah knows best.

[2] Reported by Aḥmad (442, 438, 4/437), and also Tirmidhī (3342) who said: "It is strange."

Furthermore, in its chain is a man not named. It has been reported as a statement of 'Imrān ibn Ḥuṣayn, and Ibn Kathīr preferred it to be an *athr* statement in his '*Tafsīr*' (8/415).

Also refer to '*Fatḥ Al-Bārī*' (8/702).

Imām Aḥmad and Tirmidhī also narrated it from ‘Imrān ibn Ḥusayn, from the Prophet ﷺ.

One opinion is that it refers to the creation, some of which are even, and some are odd, and the ten days are included in these creations.

Another opinion is that "*the even*" refers to all of creation and "*the odd*" refers to Allah, and the ten days are among the creations.

THE TEN WITHIN THE 40 DAYS OF MŪSĀ ﷺ

❖ Among its virtues is that it is **part of the forty days that Allah appointed for Mūsā (Moses)** ﷺ.

Allah said:

﴿ وَوَاعَدْنَا مُوسَىٰ ثَلَاثِيْنَ لَيْلَةً وَّأَتْمَمْنَاهَا بِعَشْرٍ فَتَمَّ مِيْقَاتُ رَبِّهِ أَرْبَعِيْنَ لَيْلَةً ﴾

And We appointed for Moses thirty nights and perfected them with ten more, so his Lord's appointed term of forty nights was complete. [Al-A'raf : 142]

However, there is a difference of opinion among the interpreters whether the ten days of Dhū al-Ḥijjah are the conclusion of the forty, making them the ten that completed the thirty, or whether they are the first of the forty, making them part of the thirty that were completed by ten.

‘Abd al-Razzāq narrated from Ma‘mar, from Yazīd ibn Abī Ziyād, from Mujāhid, who said: "There is no deed in the days of the year better than those in the ten days of Dhū al-Ḥijjah, and they are the ten that Allah completed for Mūsā ﷺ." [1]

---

[1] Reported by ‘Abd al-Razzāq in his ‘*Muṣannaf*' (8119), and it is *mursal* (a *ḥadīth* with a missing link).

FROM THE WELL-KNOWN MONTHS

❖ Among its virtues is that it is **the end of the "*known months*"**, the months of Ḥajj that Allah mentioned:

﴿ الْحَجُّ أَشْهُرٌ مَّعْلُومَاتٌ ﴾

Ḥajj is (in) the well-known months.
[Al-Baqarah : 197]

These are *Shawwāl, Dhā al-Qa'dah*, and ten days of Dhū al-Ḥijjah.

This was narrated from 'Umar, his son 'Abdullāh, 'Alī, Ibn Mas'ūd, Ibn 'Abbās, Ibn al-Zubayr, and others ﷺ.

It is the opinion of most of the Tābi'īn; the schools of Shāfi'ī, Aḥmad, Abū Ḥanīfah, Abū Yūsuf, and Abū Thawr, among others.

However, Shafi'i and a group excluded the Day of Sacrifice, while most included it, considering it the day of the Greater Ḥajj, in which most of the Ḥajj rituals are performed.

Some said that all of Dhū al-Ḥijjah is part of the months of Ḥajj, which is the opinion of Mālik, the old school of Shāfi'i, a narration from Ibn 'Umar, and some of the Salaf.

There is a *marfū' ḥadīth* reported by Ṭabarānī, but it is not authentic. [1]

The discussion on this matter is extensive and not the place for it here.

---

[1] Ṭabarānī reported in '*Al-Awsaṭ*' (1584) from Abū Umāmah, who said: The Messenger of Allah ﷺ said about the words of Allah: ﴿ الْحَجُّ أَشْهُرٌ مَّعْلُومَاتٌ ﴾ :

« شَوَّال وَذُو القَعْدَة وَذَو الحِجَّة »

Shawwāl, Dhū al-Qa'dah, and Dhū al-Ḥijjah.

He also reported it (7060) from Ibn 'Umar ﷺ with the same meaning.

He said in '*Majma' Al-Zawā'id*' (3/218): Ṭabarānī narrated it in '*Al-Ṣaghīr*' and '*Al-Awsaṭ*', and in it is Ḥusayn ibn Makharrāq. Ṭabarānī said: Kūfī; reliable but weakened by Dāraquṭnī, and the rest of its narrators are trustworthy.

THE DAYS OF DHIKR

❖ Among its virtues is that it is **part of the known days during which Allah has legislated His *dhikr* (remembrance) for what He has provided of livestock.**

Allah the Almighty said:

﴿ وَأَذِّن فِي النَّاسِ بِالْحَجِّ يَأْتُوكَ رِجَالًا وَعَلَىٰ كُلِّ ضَامِرٍ يَأْتِينَ مِن كُلِّ فَجٍّ عَمِيقٍ ۝ لِيَشْهَدُوا مَنَافِعَ لَهُمْ وَيَذْكُرُوا اسْمَ اللَّهِ فِي أَيَّامٍ مَّعْلُومَاتٍ عَلَىٰ مَا رَزَقَهُم مِّن بَهِيمَةِ الْأَنْعَامِ ﴾

And proclaim to the people the Ḥajj; they will come to you on foot and on every lean camel; coming from every distant pass;- So that they may be present for their benefits, and remember Allah's name during the known days upon what He has provided for them of [sacrificial] livestock animals. [Al-Ḥajj : 27-28]

The majority of scholars believe that these known days are the ten days of Dhū al-Ḥijjah; among them are Ibn 'Umar, Ibn 'Abbās, Al-Ḥasan, 'Atā', Mujāhid, 'Ikrimah, Qatādah, and Nakha'ī.

This is the opinion of Abū Ḥanīfah, Shāfi'ī, and Aḥmad in his well-known view.

It was narrated from Abū Mūsā Al-Ash'arī ﷺ that the known days are the nine days of Dhū al-Ḥijjah excluding the Day of Sacrifice, and that he said: "Supplications are not rejected during them." This was reported by Ja'far Al-Firyābī and others.

A group said that these are the days of sacrifice. This was narrated from some of the Salaf, and it is the opinion of Mālik and Abū Yūsuf.

THE DHIKR ON THE SACRIFICIAL ANIMALS

They considered the remembrance of Allah during them to be the mention [of the name of Allah] at the time of slaughter.

This is also the opinion of Ibn 'Umar ﷺ. Marwadhī narrated from Aḥmad that he approved of it.

The first opinion is more apparent.

The *dhikr* of Allah over the livestock is not restricted to the time of slaughter, as Allah the Almighty said:

﴿ كَذَلِكَ سَخَّرَهَا لَكُمْ لِتُكَبِّرُوا اللهَ عَلَى مَا هَدَاكُمْ ﴾

In this way, He has subjugated them for you that you may glorify Allah for guiding you. [Al-Ḥajj : 37]

And Almighty Allah said:

﴿ وَلِكُلِّ أُمَّةٍ جَعَلْنَا مَنْسَكًا لِيَذْكُرُوا اسْمَ اللهِ عَلَى مَا رَزَقَهُمْ مِنْ بَهِيْمَةِ الْأَنْعَامِ ﴾

And for all nations, We have appointed a rite [of sacrifice] that they may mention the name of Allah upon what He has provided for them of [sacrificial] animals.
[Al-Ḥajj : 34]

Also, Almighty Allah said after this:

﴿ فَكُلُوا مِنْهَا وَأَطْعِمُوا الْبَآئِسَ الْفَقِيرَ ۝ ثُمَّ لْيَقْضُوا تَفَثَهُمْ وَلْيُوفُوا نُذُورَهُمْ وَلْيَطَّوَّفُوا بِالْبَيْتِ الْعَتِيقِ ﴾

So eat from it and feed the needy destitute. Then let them cleanse their dirt and fulfil their vows, and let them perform Ṭawāf around the ancient House.
[Al-Ḥajj: 28-29]

Allah made all this after mentioning His remembrance in the known days, fulfilling their vows and Ṭawāf around the ancient House (the *Ka'bah*).

Ṭawāf around the House is done *on* the Day of Sacrifice and after it, but not before it.

Allah ordered this in sequence with the word *"then,"* indicating that the known days mentioned are those *before* the Day of Sacrifice (*Yawm al-Naḥr*), which are the ten days of Dhū al-Ḥijjah.

As for Allah's words:

﴿ وَيَذْكُرُوا اسْمَ اللَّهِ فِي أَيَّامٍ مَّعْلُومَاتٍ عَلَى مَا رَزَقَهُم مِّنْ بَهِيمَةِ الْأَنْعَامِ ﴾

And remember Allah's name during the known days upon what He has provided for them of [sacrificial] livestock animals. [Al-Ḥajj : 28]

It is said that it refers to mentioning Him at the time of slaughter, which occurs on the Day of Sacrifice; it is the best of the days of sacrifice.

The more correct opinion is that it refers to mentioning Him in gratitude for the blessing of subjugating livestock for His servants; for Allah has many blessings upon His servants in livestock, some of which He has enumerated in various places in the Qur'an.

Pilgrims have a particular relationship with this that others do not; they travel on them to the *Ḥaram* (Sacred Sanctuary in Makkah) to perform their rituals, as Allah the Almighty said:

﴿ وَعَلَى كُلِّ ضَامِرٍ يَأْتِينَ مِن كُلِّ فَجٍّ عَمِيقٍ ۝ ﴾

And on every lean camel; coming from every distant pass.
[Al-Ḥajj : 28]

And Allah the Almighty said:

﴿ وَتَحْمِلُ أَثْقَالَكُمْ إِلَى بَلَدٍ لَّمْ تَكُونُوا بَالِغِيهِ إِلَّا بِشِقِّ الْأَنْفُسِ ﴾

And they carry your loads to a land you could not have reached except with difficulty to yourselves. [An-Nahl : 7]

They eat from their meat, drink from their milk, and benefit from their wool, fur, and hair.

The ten days of Dhū al-Ḥijjah are particularly significant for pilgrims as it is the time when they bring their sacrificial animals, completing the virtues of Ḥajj, and they eat from its meat at the end of the ten days, which is on the Day of Sacrifice.

The best practice is to bring the sacrificial animals from the *mīqāt* (the designated stations for assuming into the state of *Iḥrām*), and they are marked and garlanded at the time of *Iḥrām*.

DHIKR & THE TALBILYAH

This coincides with the recitation of *Talbiyah*, which is part of the remembrance of Allah during the known days.

In the *ḥadīth*, it is mentioned:

« أَفْضَلُ الْحَجِّ الْعَجُّ وَالثَّجُّ »

The best Ḥajj is that in which there is much raising of the
voice in Talbiyah (al-'Ajj) and much blood sacrifice (al-Thajj). [1]

In another *ḥadīth*:

« عَجُّوا التَّكْبِيرَ عَجًّا، وَثَجُّوا الإِبِلَ ثَجًّا »

Raise your voices with Takbir abundantly
and sacrifice your camels abundantly.

Thus, the abundant remembrance of Allah during the ten days is an expression of gratitude for this blessing related to livestock, some aspects of which pertain to the pilgrim's religious duties, and some to their worldly benefits.

---

[1] Reported by Tirmidhī (827), who deemed it *gharīb* (strange), and Ibn Mājah (975). Refer to: 'Naṣb Al-Rāyah' (3/8), 'Al-Talkhīṣ Al-Ḥabīr' (2/457-458).

DHIKR & THE ḤAJJ

The best deeds are those in which Allah's remembrance is abundant, especially during Ḥajj.

Allah the Almighty commanded abundant remembrance during Ḥajj; Allah said:

﴿ فَإِذَآ أَفَضْتُم مِّنْ عَرَفَاتٍ فَاذْكُرُوا اللَّهَ عِنْدَ الْمَشْعَرِ الْحَرَامِ وَاذْكُرُوهُ كَمَا هَدَاكُمْ وَإِن كُنتُم مِّن قَبْلِهِ لَمِنَ الضَّالِّينَ ۝ ثُمَّ أَفِيضُوا مِنْ حَيْثُ أَفَاضَ النَّاسُ وَاسْتَغْفِرُوا اللَّهَ إِنَّ اللَّهَ غَفُورٌ رَّحِيمٌ ﴾

Then when you return from 'Arafāt, remember Allah near the al-Mash'ar
al-Ḥarām; and remember Him just as He has guided you, for even though you
were surely from among the deviating ones before this. Then return
from where mankind return and ask forgiveness from Allah.
Indeed, Allah is Forgiving All-Merciful.
[Al-Baqarah: 198-199]

This remembrance occurs on the tenth of Dhū al-Ḥijjah. Thereafter, Almighty Allah says:

﴿ فَاذْكُرُوا اللَّهَ كَذِكْرِكُمْ آبَاءَكُمْ أَوْ أَشَدَّ ذِكْرًا ﴾

Then remember Allah similar to your remembrance of your
forefathers, or more intense remembrance. [Al-Baqarah: 200]

This remembrance occurs on the Day of Sacrifice, which is also the conclusion of the ten days.

Then Allah commanded *dhikr* after the ten days during the specified days, which are the days of *Tashrīq*.

In the 'Sunan', it is narrated from the Prophet ﷺ, who said:

« إِنَّمَا جعل الطَّوَاف بِالْبَيْتِ ، وَالسَّعْي بَيْنَ الصَّفَا وَالْمَرْوَة ، وَرَمْي الْجِمَارِ ؛ لِإِقَامَةِ ذِكْرِ الله ﷺ »

Ṭawāf around the Sacred House, running between Ṣafā and Marwah, and the
throwing of the pebbles, (all) were ordained (solely) to establish the dhikr of Allah.[1]

---

[1] Reported by Tirmidhī (902), and Abū Dawūd (1888). Tirmidhī said: This *ḥadīth* is *Ḥasan Ṣaḥīḥ*.

In the '*Musnad*' of Imām Aḥmad, it is narrated from Mu'ādh ibn Anas: A man said: "O Messenger of Allah, which military service is greatest in reward?" He ﷺ said:

« أَكْثَرُهُمْ لله ذِكْرًا »

The one with the most remembrance of Allah.

He said: "Which of the fasting people is greatest in reward?" He ﷺ said:

« أَكْثَرُهُمْ لله ذِكْرًا »

The one with the most remembrance of Allah.

Then he mentioned prayer, *zakāt*, *Ḥajj*, and charity, each time the Messenger of Allah ﷺ said:

« أَكْثَرُهُمْ لله ذِكْرًا »

The one with the most remembrance of Allah.

Abū Bakr said: "O Abū Ḥafṣ, the people who do the *dhikr* of Allah have taken all the good."

The Messenger of Allah ﷺ said:

« أَجَل »

Yes. [1]

Ibn Al-Mubārak and Ibn Abī Al-Dunyā narrated it from other *mursal* (disconnected) sources, and in some of them, the words inlude: "Which of the pilgrims is the best?" To which he ﷺ said: "*The one with the most remembrance of Allah.*"

In others, the wording is: "Which of the pilgrims has the greatest reward?" To which he ﷺ said: "*The one with the most remembrance of Allah;*" and he mentioned the rest of the deeds in a similar way as previously mentioned.

---

[1] Reported by Aḥmad (3/438).

All these discussions mentioned pertains to the pilgrim.

THE DAYS OF DHŪ AL-ḤIJJAH & THE NON-PILGRIM

As for the people in the cities, they share with the pilgrims in the ten days of Dhū al-Ḥijjah in *dhikr* and preparing the sacrificial animals.

As for preparing the sacrificial animals, the ten days are the time for preparing the sacrifices, just as the pilgrims bring their sacrificial animals.

THE NON-PILGRIM OFFERING THE SACRIFICE

Also, they share in some aspects of *Iḥrām*; for whoever enters the ten days and intends to offer a sacrifice should not take anything from his hair or nails, as narrated by Umm Salamah ﷺ from the Prophet ﷺ. Muslim reported her *ḥadīth*:

« إِذَا دَخَلَتِ العَشْرُ وَأَرَادَ أَحَدُكُم أَن يُضَحِّيَ فَلَا يَمُسَّ مِن شَعْرِهِ وَبشرِهِ شَيْئًا »

When the ten days (of Dhū al-Ḥijjah) start and one of you intends
to offer a sacrifice, he should not touch his hair and skin at all. [1]

This was taken by Shāfiʿī, Aḥmad, and the majority of the scholars of *ḥadīth*. Some of them conditioned that the sacrificial animal be bought before the ten days, but most did not condition this.

Mālik, Abū Ḥanīfah, and many jurists disagreed with this, saying that none of these actions are disliked. They based their opinion on the *ḥadīth* of ʿĀʾishah ﷺ:

كُنْتُ أَفْتِلُ قَلَائِدَ الهَدْيِ لِرَسُولِ الله ﷺ ، فَلَا يَحْرُمُ عَلَيْهِ شَيْءٌ أَحَلَّهُ اللهُ لَهُ

---

[1] Reported by Muslim (1977).

"I used to twist the garlands for the sacrificial animals of the Messenger of Allah ﷺ, and he would not avoid anything that Allah had made lawful for him." [1]

Many of the proponents of the first opinion responded by reconciling the two *ḥadīths*; thus, the *ḥadīth* of Umm Salamah ؓ is applied to one who intends to sacrifice while remaining in his city, and the *ḥadīth* of ʿĀʾishah ؓ is applied to one who sends his sacrificial animal with someone else and remains in his city.

Ibn ʿUmar used to shave his head when he sacrificed on the Day of Sacrifice, and Aḥmad explicitly mentioned this.

THE NON-PILGRIM'S DUʿĀ & DHIKR

Scholars have differed regarding making supplications (*duʿā*) in the cities on the evening of ʿArafah.

Imām Aḥmad did not practice it but did not object to those who did because it was narrated from Ibn ʿAbbās ؓ and other companions.

As for their participation in the remembrance (*dhikr*) during the known days, it is legislated for all people to increase in the *dhikr* of Allah during the ten days, especially, as the *ḥadīth* of Ibn Umar, previously mentioned, states:

« فَأَكْثِرُوا فِيهِنَّ مِنَ التَّهْلِيلِ وَالتَّكْبِيرِ وَالتَّحْمِيدِ »

So increase in them the Tahlīl (Lā ilāha illa-llāh),
Takbīr (Allāhu Akbar), and Taḥmīd (Al-ḥamdu-lillāh).

Scholars have differed regarding whether it is prescribed to make *Takbīr* aloud and openly in the markets during the ten days.

---

[1] Reported by Muslim (1321), and Aḥmad (6/35).

Some denied it, while Aḥmad and Shāfiʻī recommended it; although Shāfiʻī specified it for when one sees the livestock, and Aḥmad recommended it generally.

Bukhārī mentioned in his 'Ṣaḥīḥ' that Ibn ʻUmar ﷺ and Abū Hurayrah ﷺ used to go out to the market during the ten days, making *Takbīr*, and the people would make *Takbīr* with them because of their *Takbīr*.

It was narrated by ʻAffān: Salām Abū Al-Mundhir narrated to us, from Ḥumayd Al-Aʻraj, from Mujāhid, who said:

"Abū Hurayrah and Ibn ʻUmar used to go to the market during the ten days and make *Takbīr*, and the people would make *Takbīr* with their *Takbīr*, and they did not go there for anything else."

Jaʻfar Al-Firyābī narrated in 'Kitāb Al-ʻĪdayn', that Is-ḥāq ibn Rāhwayh narrated to us, Jarīr narrated to us, from Yazīd ibn Abī Ziyād, who said:

I saw Saʻīd ibn Jubayr, Mujāhid, and ʻAbd al-Raḥmān ibn Abī Laylā, or two of these three, and those we saw from the jurists of the people; they used to say during the ten days:

اَللهُ أَكْبَرَ، اَللهُ أَكْبَرَ، لَا إِلهَ إِلَّا اللهُ، وَاللهُ أَكْبَرَ، اَللهُ أَكْبَرَ، وَلِلهِ الْحَمْد

Allāhu akbar, Allāhu akbar, Lā ilāha illa-llāhu, Wallāhu akbar,
Allāhu akbar, Wa lillāhi al-ḥamd.

ADVICE FOR THE NON-PILGRIM IN THESE BLESSED DAYS

Since Almighty Allah has placed in the hearts of believers a longing to see His Sacred House, and not everyone is able to visit it every year, He has made Ḥajj obligatory for those who are able to do so once in a lifetime.

He made the season of the ten days common between those who travel and those who stay. So, whoever is unable to perform Ḥajj in a year, can do deeds during the ten days at home that are better than military service, which is better than Ḥajj.

لَيَالِي الْعَشْرِ أَوْقَاتُ الْإِجَـابَة   فَبَـادِرْ رَغْبَةً تُلْحِقُ ثَـوَابَة

أَلَا لَا وَقْتَ لِلْعُمَّـالِ فِـيْـهِ   ثَـوَابُ الْخَـيْرِ أَقْـرَبُ لِلْإِصَـابَة

مِنْ أَوْقَاتِ اللَّيَـالِي الْعَشْرِ حَـقًّا   فَشَـمِّرْ وَاطْلُبَنْ فِيهَا الْإِنَـابَة

The nights of the ten are times of response ...
> *So, hasten with desire to attain its reward*
Indeed, there is no time for workers ...
> *Where the reward of goodness is closer to being attained*
Than the times of the nights of the ten truly ...
> *So, strive and seek repentance in them*

Beware of sins; for they deprive one of forgiveness during the seasons of mercy!

Marwazi narrated in '*Kitāb al-Warā*" with his chain of transmission from 'Abd al-Malik ibn 'Umayr, from a man, whether he was from the Companions or the *Tabi'īn*, that a visitor came to him in his dream during the ten days of Dhū al-Ḥijjah and said:

There is no Muslim except that he is forgiven during these days, five times each day, except for the owners of the chess pieces; they say: "He has died, what is his death?" meaning the players of chess.

So, if playing chess prevents forgiveness, then what about persisting in major sins that are unanimously agreed upon?!

طَاعَةُ اللهِ خَيْرٌ مَا لَزِمَ الْعَبْـــدُ   فَكُنْ طَائِعًا وَلَا تَعْصِيَنَّة

مَا هَلَاكُ النُّفُوسِ إِلَّا الْمَعَاصِي   فَاجْتَنِبْ مَا نَهَاكَ لَا تَقْرِبَنَّة

إِنَّ شَيْئًا هَلَاكُ نَفْسِكَ فِيهِ   يَنْبَغِي أَنْ تَصُونَ نَفْسَكَ عَنَّة

Obedience to Allah is the best thing a servant can adhere to ...
So be obedient and do not disobey Him
The destruction of souls is nothing but sins ...
So avoid what He has prohibited, do not approach it
Indeed, something that brings your destruction ...
You should protect yourself from it

Sins are the cause of distance and expulsion, just as obedience is the cause of closeness and love.

أَيُضْمِنُ لِي فَتًى تَرْكَ الْمَعَاصِي وَأُرْهِنُهُ الْكَفَالَةَ بِالْخَلَاصِ

أَطَاعَ اللهَ قَوْمٌ فَاسْتَرَاحُوا وَلَمْ يَتَجَرَّعُوا غَصَصَ الْمَعَاصِي

Can a young man guarantee for me the abandonment of sins ...
And I will pledge him the guarantee of salvation
A people obeyed Allah and found rest ...
And they did not taste the bitterness of sins

Your brothers in these days have assumed *Iḥrām*, and headed towards the Sacred House, filling the space with *Talbiyah*, *Takbīr*, *Tahlīl*, *Taḥmīd*, and glorification.

They have travelled, and we have remained; they have come close, and we have stayed afar. If we were to even have a share with them, we will be fortunate.

أَتَرَاكُمْ فِي النَّقَا وَالْمُنْحَنَى أَهْلَ سَلْعٍ تَذكرونا ذكرنا

انقَطَعْنَا وَوَصَلْتُمْ فَاعْلَمُوا وَاشْكُرُوا الْمُنْعِمَ يَا أَهْلَ مِنَى

قَدْ خَسِرْنَا وَرَبِحْتُمْ فَصَلُّوا بِفُضُولِ الرِّبْحِ مَنْ قَدْ غِبْنَا

سَارَ قَلْبِي خَلْفَ أَحْمَالِكُمْ غَيْرَ أَنَّ الْعُذْرَ عَاقَ الْبَدَنَا

مَا قَطَعْتُمْ وَادِيًا إِلَّا وَقَدْ جِئْتُهُ أَسْعَى بِأَقْدَامِ الْمُنَى

أَنَا مُذْ غِبْتُمْ عَلَى تِذْكَارِكُمْ   أَتَرَى عِنْدَكُمْ مَا عِنْدَنَا

Do you see yourselves in Al-Naqā and Al-Munḥanā ...
> *O people of Sala', do you remember us as we remember you?*

We have been cut off, and you have reached, so know ...
> *And thank the Benefactor, O people of Minā*

We have lost, and you have gained, so pray ...
> *With the surplus of profit for those who have missed*

My heart traveled behind your loads ...
> *But the excuse hindered my body*

No valley you crossed, except that ...
> *I came to it striving with the feet of desire*

Since you left, I have been in your memory ...
> *Do you have with you what we have?*

The one who stays behind due to an excuse is a partner with the traveller, and perhaps the one who stays behind in his heart surpasses those who travel with their bodies.

One of them saw in a dream on the eve of 'Arafah whilst at the place of *wuqūf* (standing), someone saying to him:

"Do you see this crowd at this place of standing? None of them have (truly) performed Ḥajj, except for a man who stayed behind from the place of *wuqūf* (and was not able to be present), but he performed Ḥajj with his intention, and thus, the (reward of the) people at the place of *wuqūf* were gifted to him."

يَا سَايِرِينَ إِلَى الْبَيْتِ الْعَتِيقِ لَقَدْ   سِرْتُمْ جُسُومًا وَسِرْنَا نَحْنُ أَرْوَاحَا

إِنَّا أَقَمْنَا عَلَى عُذْرٍ وَقَدْ رَحَلُوا   وَمَنْ أَقَامَ عَلَى عُذْرٍ كَمَنْ رَاحَا

O travellers to the Ancient House, indeed ...
> *You have traveled with your bodies, and we have traveled with our souls*

We have stayed behind due to an excuse, while they have departed ...
> *And the one who stays behind due to an excuse is like the one who has travelled*

Take advantage! Take advantage; of the opportunity in these great days, for there is no substitute for them, nor are they replaceable.

Hasten! Hasten to work, and hurry! Hurry before the attack of the inevitable end, before the negligent regrets what they have done; before they ask for a return to do good deeds and are not granted what they ask for; before death intervenes between the hopeful and reaching their hope; before a person becomes bound in their grave by what they have done.

لَيْسَ لِلْمَيِّتِ فِي قَبْرِهِ فِطْرٌ وَلَا أَضْحَى وَلَا عَشْرُ

نَاءَ عَنِ الْأَهْلِ عَلَى قُرْبِهِ كَذَاكَ مَنْ مَسْكَنُهُ الْقَبْرُ

For the deceased in their grave ...
There is no ‘Īd al-Fiṭr, nor ‘Īd al-Aḍḥā, and no ten days
Distant from family despite their nearness ...
Just like one whose dwelling is the grave

O you whose grey dawn has risen after reaching forty! O you upon whom ten more years have passed after that until reaching fifty! O you who is in the throes of death between sixty and seventy! What do you await after this news except for certainty (death)?

O you whose sins are as numerous as the even and the odd! Do you not feel ashamed of the honourable scribes? Or are you among those who deny the religion?

O you whose heart's darkness is like the night when it journeys! Is it not time for your heart to be illuminated or softened?

Seek the breezes of your Lord in these ten days; for indeed, Allah has breezes in them that He bestows upon whom He wills. Whoever is touched by them will be happy for the rest of time.

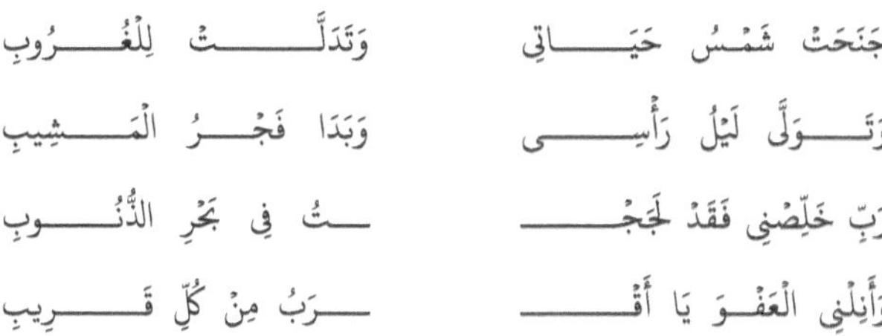

The sun of my life has leaned ...
  And descended toward setting
The night of my hair has passed ...
  And the dawn of grey has appeared
My Lord, save me for I have plunged ...
  Into the sea of sins
Grant me pardon, O You Who is ...
  Nearer than every near one

AL-MAJLIS AL-THĀNĪ:
THE VIRTUE OF THE DAY OF 'ARAFAH
& THE FESTIVAL OF SACRIFICE

In the two 'Ṣaḥīḥ's (Bukhārī and Muslim), it is narrated from 'Umar ibn al-Khaṭṭāb ﷺ, that a man from the Jews said to him:

"O Commander of the Faithful, there is a verse in your Book which, if it had been revealed to us Jews, we would have taken that day as a festival."

'Umar ﷺ asked, "Which verse?" He replied,

﴿ ٱلۡيَوۡمَ أَكۡمَلۡتُ لَـكُمۡ دِينَكُمۡ وَأَتۡمَمۡتُ عَلَيۡكُمۡ نِعۡمَتِي وَرَضِيتُ لَكُمُ ٱلۡإِسۡلَامَ دِينًا ﴾

Today, I have perfected for you your Religion, and I have completed My favour upon you, and I have chosen Islam as a religion for you.
[Al-Mā'idah : 3]

'Umar ﷺ said, "I know the day and the place where it was revealed. It was revealed while the Messenger of Allah ﷺ was standing in 'Arafah on a Friday." [1]

---

[1] Reported by Bukhārī (45), Muslim (3017), and Nasā'ī (8, 5/251 / 114).

Tirmidhī narrated from Ibn 'Abbās ﷺ something similar, and he said: It was revealed on a day of *'Īd*, a Friday, and the Day of 'Arafah. [1]

The *'Īd* is a season of joy and happiness, and the joy and happiness of the believers in this world are with their Lord when they achieve the completion of His obedience and obtain the reward for their deeds by their trust in His promise of His grace and forgiveness, as Allah Almighty says:

﴿ قُلْ بِفَضْلِ اللهِ وَبِرَحْمَتِهِ فَبِذَٰلِكَ فَلْيَفْرَحُوا هُوَ خَيْرٌ مِّمَّا يَجْمَعُونَ ﴾

Say: 'By Allah's Grace and by His mercy; so upon this they should rejoice;
it is better than what they accumulate.'
[Yūnus : 58]

One of the *'ulamā'* said: No one rejoices in anything other than Allah except because of their heedlessness of Allah; the heedless rejoice in their amusement and desires, and the wise rejoice in their Lord.

وَكَانَ فُؤَادِى خَالِيًا قَبْلَ حُبِّكُمْ   وَكَانَ بِذِكْرِ الْخَلْقِ يَلْهُو وَيَمْرَحُ

فَلَمَّا دَعَا قَلْبِى هَوَاكَ أَجَابَهُ   فَلَسْتُ أَرَاهُ عَنْ فِنَائِكَ يَبْرَحُ

رُمِيتُ بِبُعْدٍ مِّنْكَ إِنْ كُنْتُ كَاذِبًا   وَإِنْ كُنْتُ فِي الدُّنْيَا بِغَيْرِكَ أَفْرَحُ

وَإِنْ كَانَ شَىْءٌ فِي الْبِلَادِ بِأَسْرِهَا   إِذَا غِبْتَ عَنْ عَيْنِي لَعَيْنِي يَمْلَحُ

فَإِنْ شِئْتَ وَاصِلْنِي وَإِنْ شِئْتَ لَا تَصِلْ   فَلَسْتُ أَرَى قَلْبِي لِغَيْرِكَ يَصْلَحُ

My heart was empty before your love ...
> *And it used to delight and frolic in the mention of others*
But when your love called to my heart, it responded ...
> *And I do not see it departing from your courtyard*
May I be cast away from you if I am lying ...
> *And if I find joy in this world without you*

---

[1] Reported by Tirmidhī (3044), and he said: It is a *ḥasan* and *gharīb ḥadīth* from Ibn 'Abbās ﷺ, and it is authentic.

And if there is anything in the entire world ...
That would bring pleasure to my eyes if you are absent from my sight
So if you wish, keep in touch with me or if you wish, do not ...
for I do not see my heart suitable for anyone but you

When the Prophet ﷺ arrived in Madīnah, they had two days in which they used to play, so he said:

« إِنَّ اللهَ قَدْ أَبْدَلَكُمْ يَوْمَيْنِ خَيْرًا مِنْهُمَا ؛ يَوْمَ الفِطْرِ ، وَالأَضْحَى »

Allah has replaced these two days for you with something better;
the Day of Fiṭr and the Day of Aḍḥā. [1]

Allah replaced for this *Ummah* the days of play and amusement with the days of remembrance, gratitude, forgiveness, and pardon.

In this world, the believers have three *'Īds*:

* ❖ One that recurs every week,
* ❖ And two that come once each year, without repetition within the year.

EVERY FRIDAY IS A WEEKLY 'ĪD

As for the recurring *'Īd*, it is the day of Friday, which is the weekly *'Īd*. It is associated with the completion of the obligatory prayers; for Allah, the Almighty, has ordained for the believers five prayers every day and night, and the days of this world revolve around seven days.

Whenever a week completes its cycle, and the Muslims have completed their prayers within it.

It is prescribed for them on their day of completion - which is the day:

* ❖ The Creation was completed;

---

[1] Reported by Aḥmad (250, 235, 178, 3/103), and Nasā'ī (3/179).

❖ The day Ādam ﷺ was created, entered Paradise, and was expelled from it;

❖ The day the world will end and the Hour will be established;

❖ The day for gathering to listen to the remembrance and sermon, and for the Friday prayer;

- and He made it an *'Īd* for them. Hence, it is forbidden to fast on this day exclusively.

SOME VIRTUES OF JUMU'AH (FRIDAY)

Attending the Friday prayer has a resemblance to Ḥajj, and it is narrated that it is the Ḥajj of the poor.

Sa'īd ibn al-Musayyib said: Attending the Friday prayer is more beloved to me than a voluntary Ḥajj.

Arriving early for it takes the place of offering a sacrifice according to the precedence; the first is like the one who offers a camel, then a cow, then a sheep, then a chicken, then an egg.

Attending the Friday prayer necessitates the expiation of sins until the next Friday, if major sins are avoided between the two Fridays, just as an accepted Ḥajj expiates the sins of that year until the next Ḥajj.

It is narrated:

» إِذَا سَلِمَت الْجُمُعَةُ سَلِمَت الأَيَّامُ «

If the Friday is sound, the (remaining) days will be sound. [1]

It is also narrated:

» إِنَّ اللهَ تَعَالَى يَغْفِرُ يَوْمَ الْجُمُعَةِ لِكُلِّ مُسْلِمٍ «

---

[1] Reported by Ibn 'Adiy in '*Al-Kāmil*' (6/504), Ibn Ḥibbān in '*Al-Majruḥīn*' (2/123), and Abū Nu'aym in '*Al-Ḥilyah*' (7/140), and it is weak.

Indeed, Allah forgives every Muslim on Friday. [1]

In an authentic *ḥadīth*, the Prophet ﷺ said:

« مَا طَلَعَت الشَّمْسُ وَلَا غَرَبَتْ عَلَى يَوْمٍ أَفْضَلُ مِن يَوْمِ الْجُمُعَةِ »

The sun has not risen nor set on a day better than Friday. [2]

In the '*Musnad*', it is narrated that he ﷺ said about Friday:

«هو أفضل عند الله من يوم الفطر ويوم الأضحى»

*It is better with Allah than
the Day of Fiṭr and the Day of Aḍḥā.* [3]

This is the weekly *'Īd*, and it is related to the completion of the obligatory prayers, which are the greatest pillars of Islam after the two testimonies of faith.

As for the two *'Īds* that do not recur every year, but each comes once in the year:

THE '*ĪD AL-FIṬR*

One of them is the *'Īd al-Fiṭr* after the fasting of *Ramaḍān*.

It is associated with the completion of fasting *Ramaḍān*, which is the fourth pillar of Islam.

---

[1] Reported by Ṭabarānī in '*Al-Awsaṭ*' (4817) from the *ḥadīth* of Anas ؇; and reported by Khaṭīb in his '*Tārikh*' (6/46) from the *ḥadīth* of Abū Hurayrah ؇.

[2] Reported by Tirmidhī (3339), and he indicated towards some weakness in its chain, but its meaning is confirmed from the *ḥadīth* of Abū Hurayrah ؇ in Muslim (854) with the wording:

« خَيْرُ يَوْمٍ طَلَعَتْ عَلَيْهِ الشَّمْسُ يَوْمَ الْجُمُعَةِ ... »

"The best day on which the sun has risen is Friday..."

[3] Musnad Imām Aḥmad (3/430).

When Muslims complete their obligatory fasting of the month, and earn Allah's forgiveness and deliverance from the fire, as fasting leads to the forgiveness of past sins, and at its end, there is deliverance from the fire for those who deserved it due to their sins.

Allah has prescribed for them, after completing their fasting, a festival where they gather to thank Allah, remember Him, and glorify Him for guiding them.

On this *ʿĪd*, prayer and charity are prescribed.

It is a day of rewards where the fasting people receive the reward for their fasting and return from their *ʿĪd* with forgiveness.

THE ʿĪD AL-AḌHĀ & THE DAY OF ʿARAFAH

The second *ʿĪd* is *ʿĪd al-Aḍḥā*, which is the greater and better of the two *ʿĪds*.

It is associated with the completion of Ḥajj, which is the fifth pillar of Islam. When Muslims complete their Ḥajj, they are forgiven.

Ḥajj is completed by the Day of ʿArafah and standing in ʿArafah, as it is the greatest pillar of Ḥajj, as the Prophet ﷺ said:

« الحـجّ عرفة »

Ḥajj is ʿArafah. [1]

The Day of ʿArafah is the day of deliverance from the fire, where Allah frees those standing in ʿArafah and those from the cities of Muslims who did not stand there. Thus, the day following it becomes a festival for all Muslims in all their cities; for those who attended the

---

[1] Reported by Aḥmad (335, 310, 4/309), Abū Dawūd (1949), Tirmidhī (889), Ibn Mājah (3015), and Nasāʾī (264, 5/256).

Abū Dawūd said: This *ḥadīth* is a fundamental principle.

season and those who did not, sharing in the deliverance and forgiveness on the Day of 'Arafah.

Muslims do not all participate in Ḥajj every year as a mercy and ease from Allah upon His servants, as He made Ḥajj an obligation of a lifetime, not an annual obligation.

However, it is a communal obligation every year, unlike fasting, which is an annual obligation on every Muslim.

When the Day of 'Arafah is completed and Allah frees His believing servants from the fire, all Muslims share in the 'Īd following that.

It is prescribed for all to draw near to Him with sacrifices, which is the shedding of the blood of the sacrificial animals.

The people performing Ḥajj throw the stones, begin to exit their state of Iḥrām, groom themselves, fulfil their vows, and offer their sacrifices. Then they perform ṭawāf around the Ancient House.

The people in the cities gather to remember Allah, glorify Him, and perform the prayer.

Mukhannaf ibn Sulaym, who is counted among the Companions, said: Going out on the Day of Fiṭr equals an 'Umrah, and going out on the Day of Aḍḥā equals a Ḥajj.

Then they perform their sacrificial rites and offer their sacrifices by shedding the blood of their offerings; this is their way of giving thanks for these blessings.

The prayer and sacrifice combined on 'Īd al-Aḍḥā are better than the prayer and charity on 'Īd al-Fiṭr.

For this reason, the Messenger of Allah ﷺ was commanded to give thanks to his Lord for granting him al-Kawthar by praying to his Lord and sacrificing, and he was told:

﴿ قُلْ إِنَّ صَلَاتِي وَنُسُكِي وَمَحْيَايَ وَمَمَاتِي لِلَّهِ رَبِّ الْعَلَمِينَ ﴾

Say: 'My Prayer, my rites of sacrifice, my living and
my dying certainly belong to Allah, Lord of the worlds'
[Al-Anʿām : 162]

Hence, the command to recite this verse when slaughtering the sacrifices.

The sacrifices are the tradition of Ibrāhīm ﷺ and Muḥammad ﷺ.

For Allah prescribed them to Ibrāhīm ﷺ when He ransomed his son, whom he was commanded to sacrifice, with a great sacrifice.

In the *ḥadīth* of Zayd ibn Arqam: It was said: "O Messenger of Allah, what are these sacrifices?"

He ﷺ said: "*The tradition of Ibrāhīm ﷺ.*" He was asked: "What do we get from them?"

He ﷺ said: "*For every hair, a good deed.*" He was asked: "What about wool?"

He ﷺ said: "*For every hair of wool, a good deed.*" Reported by Ibn Mājah and others. [1]

These are the festivals of Muslims in this world, and all of them occur upon the completion of obedience to their Lord, al-Malik (The Sovereign) al-Wahhāb (The Bestower), and their attainment of the reward and recompense He promised them.

أَلَا تَعْطِفُ عَلَيَّ أَلَا تَجُـــــــــودُ   بِحُرْمَةِ غُرْبَتِي كَمْ ذَا الصَّـــــــدُودِ

وَحُزْنِي فِي ازْدِيَادٍ لَا يَبِـــــــيدُ   سُرُورُ الْعِيدِ قَدْ عَمَّ النَّـــــوَاحِي

فَعُذْرِي فِي الْهَوَى أَن لَّا أَعُـــــــودُ   فَإِنْ كُنْتُ اقْتَرَفْتُ خِلَالَ سُـــــــوْءٍ

By the sanctity of my estrangement, how much rejection ...
> *Will you not show compassion to me, will you not be generous?*

The joy of 'Īd has spread to all regions ...
> *But my sorrow is increasing, it does not vanish*

If I have committed any sins ...
> *My excuse in love is that I will not return to them*

Another recited:

---

[1] Reported by Aḥmad (4/368) and Ibn Mājah (3127).

وَأَنَا فَقِيرٌ وَحِيدُ   لِلنَّاسِ عَشْرٌ وَعِيدُ

قَدْ لَذَّ لِي مَا تُرِيدُ   يَا غَايَتِي وَمُنَائَى

For the people, there are the tenth and the 'Īd …
    And I am a poor, lonely one
O my goal and my desire …
    What you want has delighted me

Al-Shibli recited:

وَانْتِظَارُ الْأَمِيرِ وَالسُّلْطَانِ   لَيْسَ عِيدُ الْمُحِبِّ قَصْدُ الْمُصَلَّى

بِّ كَرِيمًا مُقَرَّبًا فِي أَمَانِ   إِنَّمَا الْعِيدُ أَنْ تَكُونَ لَدَى الْحُـ

The 'Īd for the lover is not going to the prayer ground …
    And waiting for the prince and the sultan
The 'Īd is to be with the beloved …
    Honoured, close, and in peace

Another recited:

فَمَا أَصْنَعُ بِالْعِيدِ   إِذَا مَا كُنْتَ لِي عِيدًا

كَجَرْيِ الْمَاءِ فِي الْعُودِ   جَرَى حُبُّكَ فِي قَلْبِي

If you are not my 'Īd …
    Then what will I do with the 'Īd?
Your love has flowed in my heart …
    Like the flow of water in wood

Another recited:

فَقُلْتُ خِلْعَةً سَاقَ حُسْنُهُ بِرْعَا   قَالُوا غَدًا الْعِيدِ مَاذَا أَنْتَ لَابِسُهُ

قَلْبٌ يَرَى إِلْفَهُ الْأَعْيَادَ وَالْجُمَعَا   صَبْرٌ وَفَقْرُهُمَا ثَوْبَانِ تَحْتَهُمَا

يَوْمَ التَّزَاوُرِ فِي الثَّوْبِ الَّذِي خَلَعَا   أَحْرَى الْمَلَابِسِ أَنْ تَلْقَى الْحَبِيبَ بِهِ

الدَّهْرُ لِي مَأْتَمٌ إِنْ غِبْتَ يَا أَمَلِي وَالْعِيدُ مَا كُنْتَ لِي مَرْأًى وَّمُسْتَمَعَا

They said tomorrow is ʿĪd, what will you wear ...

I said a garment with its beauty blooming

Patience and poverty are two garments beneath them ...

A heart that sees its companion in ʿĪd and gatherings

The best clothes to meet the beloved with ...

On the day of visit in the garment they abandoned

The time is a mourning for me if you are absent, O my hope ...

And the ʿĪd is when you are my sight and hearing

As for the festivals of the believers in Paradise, they are the days they visit their Lord, the Almighty.

They visit Him and He honours them with the utmost honour and manifests Himself to them, and they look at Him. Nothing He gives them is more beloved to them than that.

It is the increase that Allah mentioned:

﴿ لِلَّذِينَ اَحْسَنُوا الْحُسْنٰى وَزِيَادَةٌ ﴾

For those who have done good there is the best reward and more.

[Yūnus : 26].

The lover has no ʿĪd except the closeness of his beloved.

إِنَّ يَوْمًا جَـــــــامِعًا شملِي بِهِمْ ذَاكَ عِيدٌ لَيْسَ لِي عِيدٌ سِـــــــوَاهُ

Indeed, a day that gathers me with them ...

That is the ʿĪd, there is no ʿĪd for me other than that

Every day that was an ʿĪd for the Muslims in this world will be an ʿĪd for them in Paradise, where they gather to visit their Lord, and He manifests Himself to them.

The day of Friday is called in Paradise the Day of *Mazīd* (Increase), and the days of *Fiṭr* and *Aḍḥā* are days the people of Paradise gather for the visit.

It is narrated that women join men in these days, just as they used to attend the two ʿĪds with men, but not Friday.

This is for the general people of Paradise, but as for their elite, every day is an ʿĪd for them.

They visit their Lord twice every day, morning and evening.

For the elite, all the days of the world were ʿĪds, so all their days in the Hereafter have become ʿĪds.

عِيدِى مُقِيمٌ وَّعِيدُ النَّاسِ مُنْصَرِفُ   وَالْقَلْبُ مِنِّى عَنِ اللَّذَاتِ مُنْحَرِفُ

وَلِى قَرِينَانِ مَا لِى مِنْهُمَا خَلَفُ   طُول الْحَنِينِ وَعَيْن دَمِعِهَا يَكِفُ

My ʿĪd is permanent while the people's ʿĪd is fleeting ...
And my heart has turned away from pleasures
I have two companions, from whom I have no escape ...
Long yearning and an eye that sheds tears

Since ʿĪd al-Aḍḥā is the greater and better of the two ʿĪds, and it combines the honour of place and time for the people performing Ḥajj, they have with it other ʿĪds before and after it; before it is the Day of ʿArafah, and after it are the Days of *Tashrīq*.

All these days are ʿĪds for the people performing Ḥajj, as in the *ḥadīth* of ʿUqbah ibn ʿĀmir from the Prophet ﷺ, who said:

« يَوْمُ عَرَفَةَ ، يَوْم النَّحْرِ ، وَأَيَّام التَّشْرِيقِ عِيدُنَا أَهْلَ الإِسْلَامِ ، وَهِيَ أَيَّامُ أَكْلٍ وَشُرْبٍ »

The Day of ʿArafah, the Day of Sacrifice, and the Days of Tashrīq are our ʿĪd,
the people of Islam, and they are days of eating and drinking.

The people of the *Sunan* reported it, and Tirmidhī authenticated it. [1]

For this reason, it is not prescribed for the people performing Ḥajj to fast on the Day of ʿArafah; because it is the first of their ʿĪds and their greatest gatherings. The Prophet ﷺ did not keep this fast at

---

[1] Reported by Aḥmad (4/152), Abū Dawūd (2419), Tirmidhī (773), and Nasāʾī (5/252).

'Arafah at a moment wherein the people were all observant of him. It is narrated that he forbade fasting on the Day of 'Arafah at 'Arafah.

It is narrated from Sufyān ibn 'Uyaynah that he was asked about the prohibition of fasting on the Day of 'Arafah at 'Arafah, and he said:

Because they are the visitors and guests of Allah, and it is not appropriate for the generous to make his guests go hungry.

This meaning is also found in the two ʿĪds and the Days of *Tashrīq*; for all people in these days are the guests of Allah, the Almighty, especially on ʿĪd al-Aḍḥā; as people eat from the meat of their sacrifices, both those at 'Arafah and others.

The three Days of *Tashrīq* are also days of ʿĪd, and for this reason, the Prophet, ﷺ, sent someone to announce in Makkah:

« إنها أيام أكل وشرب وذكر الله ﷻ ، فلا يصو منّ أحد »

They are days of eating, drinking, and remembering
Allah, the Almighty, so no one should fast.

THE PERFECTION OF ISLAM REVEALED
ON THE DAY OF 'ARAFAH

Two ʿĪds may coincide on one day, as when Friday coincides with the Day of 'Arafah or the Day of *Naḥr* (Sacrifice), increasing the sanctity and virtue of that day due to the combination of two ʿĪds.

This happened to the Prophet, ﷺ, in his Ḥajj, as the Day of 'Arafah was on a Friday, and on that day this verse was revealed:

﴿ ٱلۡيَوۡمَ أَكۡمَلۡتُ لَـكُمۡ دِيۡنَكُمۡ وَأَتۡمَمۡتُ عَلَيۡكُمۡ نِعۡمَتِيۡ وَرَضِيۡتُ لَـكُمُ ٱلۡإِسۡلَامَ دِيۡنًا ﴾

Today, I have perfected for you your Religion, and I have completed My favour
upon you, and I have chosen Islam as a religion for you.
[Al-Mā'idah : 3]

The completion of the religion on that day was achieved in several ways:

❖ One of them is that the Muslims had not yet performed the obligatory Ḥajj after it was prescribed, not any one of them; this is the opinion of most scholars or many of them. Thus, their religion was completed by **fulfilling all the pillars of Islam.**

❖ Another way is that Allah **restored Ḥajj upon the principles of Ibrāhīm 🕮 and eliminated polytheism and its people,** so none of them mingled with the Muslims at that site.

Sha'bī said: This verse was revealed to the Prophet 🕮 while he was standing in 'Arafah, at the position of Ibrāhīm 🕮. Polytheism had vanished, the monuments of ignorance had been demolished, and no one circled the Ka'bah naked.

The same was said by Qatādah and others.

It has been said that no permissibility or prohibition was revealed after it. This was stated by Abū Bakr ibn 'Ayyāsh.

THE COMPLETION OF ALLAH'S FAVOUR REVEALED ON THE DAY OF 'ARAFAH

As for the completion of the favour, it was achieved **through forgiveness,** for the favour is not complete without it, as He said to His Prophet 🕮:

﴿ لِيَغْفِرَ لَكَ اللَّهُ مَا تَقَدَّمَ مِنْ ذَنْبِكَ وَمَا تَأَخَّرَ وَيُتِمَّ نِعْمَتَهُ عَلَيْكَ وَيَهْدِيَكَ صِرَاطًا مُسْتَقِيمًا ﴾

So that Allah may forgive for you 🕮 what has gone before of your shortfalls and
what is to come, and He may complete His favour upon you
and guide you to the straight path.
[Al-Fatḥ : 2]

And Allah said in the verse of ablution:

$$ ﴿ وَلَـٰكِنْ يُرِيدُ لِيُطَهِّرَكُمْ وَلِيُتِمَّ نِعْمَتَهُ عَلَيْكُمْ ﴾ $$

Rather He intends to purify you and to complete His favour upon you
[Al-Māʼidah : 6]

From here, Muḥammad ibn Kaʻb al-Quraẓī derived that ablution expiates sins, as explicitly stated in the *Sunnah*.

It is also supported by the *ḥadīth* that the Prophet ﷺ heard a man praying and saying:

$$ اَللَّهُمَّ إِنِّى أَسْأَلُكَ تَمَامَ النِّعْمَةِ $$

O Allah, I ask You for the completion of the favour.

He ﷺ said to him:

$$ « تَمَامُ النِّعْمَةِ النَّجَاةُ مِنَ النَّارِ، وَدُخُولُ الْجَنَّةِ » $$

The completion of the favour is
deliverance from the fire and entry into Paradise. [1]

Thus, this verse bears witness to what is narrated about the Day of ʻArafah, that it is the day of forgiveness and deliverance from the fire.

SOME VIRTUES OF THE DAY OF ʻARAFAH

The Day of Arafah has numerous virtues:

- ❖ One of them is that it is **the day of the completion of the religion and the perfection of the favour.**

---

[1] Reported by Aḥmad (5/231), and Tirmidhī (3527).

❖ Another is that **it is an *ʿĪd* for the people of Islam**, as stated by ʿUmar ibn al-Khaṭṭāb ﷺ and Ibn ʿAbbās ﷺ.

Ibn ʿAbbās ﷺ said: "It was revealed on a day of two *ʿĪds*; a Friday and the Day of ʿArafah." [1]

It is narrated from ʿUmar ﷺ that he said: "Both are *ʿĪds* for us, praise be to Allah." [2]

This is supported by the *ḥadīth* of ʿUqbah ibn ʿĀmir mentioned earlier, but it is an *ʿĪd* specifically for those at the standing. Fasting on this day is prescribed for the people of the cities according to the majority of scholars, although some of the predecessors differed.

❖ Another virtue is that it is said to be **the *"even"* that Allah swore by in His Book**, and that the "odd" is the Day of *Naḥr* (Sacrifice).

This is narrated from the Prophet, ﷺ, from the *ḥadīth* of Jābir ﷺ. Reported by Imām Aḥmad and Nasāʾī in his *'al-Kubrā'*. [3]

❖ It is also said to be **the *"witnessed day"* that Allah swore by in His Book**, as He said:

$$﴿ وَشَاهِدٍ وَّمَشْهُودٍ ﴾$$

And [by] the witness and witnessed!
[Al-Burūj : 3]

In *'Musnad'*, it is narrated from Abū Hurayrah ﷺ, both *marfūʿ* and *mawqūf*: *"The witness is the Day of Arafah, and the witnessed is the Day of Friday."* [4]

Tirmidhī reported it as *marfūʿ*.

---

[1] Reported by Ibn Jarir in his Tafsir (6/82).
[2] Reported by Ibn Jarir in his Tafsir (6/83).
[3] Reported by Aḥmad (3/327) and Nasāʾī in *'Al-Kubrā'* (11608, 4086).
[4] Reported by Aḥmad (2/298); and also Tirmidhī (3339), who indicated towards its weakness.

It is also narrated from 'Alī ﷺ as his statement.

Ṭabarānī reported from the *ḥadīth* of 'Abū Mālik al-Ash'arī as *marfu'*: *"The witness is the Day of Friday, and the witnessed is the Day of Arafah."* [1]

Hence, if the Day of Arafah coincides with a Friday, both the witness and the witnessed occur on the same day.

❖ Another virtue is that it is narrated to be **the best of days**.

This is reported by Ibn Ḥibbān in his *'Ṣaḥīḥ'*, from the *ḥadīth* of Jābir ﷺ, from the Prophet ﷺ who said:

« أفضل الأيام يوم عرفة »

The best of days is the Day of Arafah.

This is the opinion of a group of scholars.

Others said that the Day of *Naḥr* (Sacrifice) is the best of days; based on the *ḥadīth* of 'Abdullāh ibn Qurṭ from the Prophet ﷺ, who said:

« أعظم الأيام عند الله يوم النّحر ، ثم يوم القرّ »

The greatest of days with Allah is the Day of Sacrifice, then the Day of Rest. [2]

Reported by Imām Aḥmad, Abū Dāwūd, Nasā'ī, and Ibn Ḥibbān in his *'Ṣaḥīḥ'* with the wording: *"The best of days."*

❖ Another virtue is that it is narrated from Anas ibn Mālik ﷺ that he said: "It used to be said: **The Day of Arafah is worth ten thousand days in virtue.**"

This has been mentioned in the virtue of the ten days.

---

[1] Reported by Ṭabarānī in '*Al-Kabīr*' (3458).
[2] Reported by Aḥmad (4/350) and Abū Dawūd (1765).

It is also narrated from 'Aṭā' that he said: Whoever fasts on the Day of Arafah, it is as if he fasted two thousand days.

❖ Another virtue is that it is considered the day of the *al-Ḥajj al-Akbar* (Greatest Ḥajj). [1]

This is according to a group of the predecessors, including 'Umar ﷺ and others.

Others disagreed, saying that the Day of the Greater Ḥajj is the Day of Sacrifice.

This is also narrated from the Prophet ﷺ. [2]

❖ Another virtue is that **fasting on it is an expiation for two years,** and we will mention the *ḥadīth* about this later, *in-shā'-Allāh*.

❖ Another virtue is that it is **a day of forgiveness of sins, pardon, deliverance from the fire, and boasting about the people at the standing.**

As in '*Ṣaḥīḥ Muslim*', from 'Ā'ishah ﷺ, from the Prophet ﷺ who said:

« مَا مِنْ يَوْمٍ أَكْثَرَ مِنْ أَنْ يُعْتِقَ اللهُ فِيهِ عَبِيدًا مِنَ النَّارِ مِنْ يَوْمِ عَرَفَةَ ، وَإِنَّهُ لَيَدْنُو ، ثُمَّ يُبَاهِي بِهِمُ الْمَلَائِكَة ، فَيَقُولُ : مَا أَرَادَ هَؤُلَاءِ ؟ »

There is no day on which Allah frees more servants from the Fire than the Day of 'Arafah. He draws near, then He boasts about them to the angels, saying: "What do these want?" [3]

---

[1] This is narrated as *marfu'*, mentioned by Ibn 'Abd al-Barr in '*al-Tamhīd*' (1/126) without a chain.
[2] Reported by Tirmidhī (957-958), who preferred its *mawqūf* form on 'Alī ﷺ. Refer to '*Al-Tamhīd*' by Ibn 'Abd al-Barr (1/125) and '*Ṣaḥīḥ Muslim*' (4/107).
[3] Reported by Muslim (1348) and Nasā'ī (5/251-252).

In '*Al-Musnad*', it is narrated from 'Abdullāh ibn 'Amr, from the Prophet ﷺ, who said:

«إِنَّ اللهَ تَعَالَى يُبَاهِي مَلَائِكَتَهُ عَشِيَّةَ عَرَفَة ، فَيَقُولُ : انْظُرُوا إِلَى عِبَادِي ، أَتَوْنِي شُعْثًا غُبْرًا»

Indeed, Allah boasts to His angels on the afternoon of Arafah, saying:
"Look at My servants; they have come to Me dishevelled and dusty."[1]

It is also reported in it ('*Musnad Aḥmad*'), from Abū Hurayrah ﷺ, from the Prophet ﷺ, who said:

«إِنَّ اللهَ يُبَاهِي بِأَهْلِ عَرَفَات ، يَقُولُ: انْظُرُوا إِلَى عِبَادِي شُعْثًا غُبْرًا»

Indeed, Allah boasts about the people of 'Arafāt, saying:
"Look at My servants, they have come to Me disheveled and dusty."

This is reported by Ibn Ḥibbān in his '*Ṣaḥīḥ*'.[2]

He also reported from the *ḥadīth* of Jābir ﷺ from the Prophet ﷺ, who said:

«مَا مِن يَوْمٍ أَفْضَلُ عِنْدَ الله مِنْ يَوْمِ عَرَفَةَ ، يَنْزِلُ اللهَ ﷻ إِلَى السَّمَاءِ الدُّنْيَا فَيُبَاهِي بِأَهْلِ الأَرْضِ أَهْلَ السَّمَاءِ ، فَيَقُولُ : انْظُرُوا إِلَى عِبَادِي شُعْثًا غُبْرًا ضَاحِينَ ، جَاءُوا مِنْ كُلِّ فَجٍّ عَمِيقٍ ، يَرْجُونَ رَحْمَتِي وَلَمْ يَرَوْا عَذَابِي ؛ فَلَمْ يَرَ أَكْثَرَ عَتِيقًا مِنَ النَّارِ مِنْ يَوْمِ عَرَفَةَ»

There is no day better in the sight of Allah than the Day of 'Arafah.
Allah, the Blessed and Exalted, descends to the lowest heaven and boasts
about the people of the earth to the people of the heaven, saying:
"Look at My servants; they have come to Me disheveled and dusty,
smiling, coming from every deep valley. They hope for My mercy
and have not seen My punishment."

---

[1] Reported by Aḥmad (2/224).
[2] Reported by Aḥmad (2/305), Ibn Khuzaymah (2839), Ibn Ḥibbān (3852), Ḥākim (1/465), and Bayhaqī (5/58).

There is no day on which more people are freed
from the Fire than the Day of 'Arafah. [1]

Ibn Mandah reported it in *'Kitāb al-Tawḥīd'* with the wording: *"When it is the Day of 'Arafah, Allah descends to the lowest heaven and boasts about them to the angels, saying:*

'Look at My servants; they have come to Me disheveled and dusty from every deep valley. I bear witness to you that I have forgiven them.'

The angels say: 'O Lord, so-and-so is burdened with sins.'

He says: 'I have forgiven them.'

There is no day on which more people are freed from the Fire than the Day of 'Arafah." [2]

We have also related it from another chain of transmission with an addition in it of:

$$ \text{« أُشْهِدُكُمْ يَا عِبَادِي أَنِّي قَدْ غَفَرْتُ لِمُحْسِنِهِم ، وَتَجَاوَزْتُ عَنْ مُسِيئِهِم »} $$

I make you witness, O My servants, that I have forgiven the
righteous among them and overlooked the wrongdoers.

We have also related it from the narration of Ismā'īl ibn Rāfi'- and he has been critiqued - from Anas ﷺ, from the Prophet ﷺ who said:

"Allah descends to the lowest heaven on the afternoon of 'Arafah, then boasts about you to the angels, saying:

'These are My servants, they have come to Me disheveled from every deep valley, hoping for My mercy and forgiveness. If their sins were as numerous as the grains of sand, I would forgive them.

---

[1] Reported by Ibn Ḥibbān (3853), and Abū Ya'lā al-Mawṣilī in his *'Musnad'* (2090). [Refer to: *'Majma' al-Zawā'id'* (3/253).

[2] Reported by Ibn Khuzaymah (2840) through the chain of Marzūq Abū Bakr, the freed slave of Ṭalḥah al-Bāhilī, from Abū al-Zubayr, from Jābir ﷺ. Then he said: "I disavow the responsibility for Marzuq." He said: "The chain is good and connected."

Pour forth, My servants, (in a state that your sins have been) forgiven for you and (also for) those for whom you intercede." [1]

Bazzār reported it in his '*Musnad*' with the same meaning, from the *ḥadīth* of Mujāhid, from Ibn 'Umar, from the Prophet ﷺ.

He said: We do not know a chain better than this transmission.

Ṭabarānī and others reported it from the *ḥadīth* of 'Abdullāh ibn 'Amr bin Al-'Āṣ ﷺ, from the Prophet ﷺ, in a summarised form.

We also narrated it from the route of Al-Walīd ibn Muslim, who said: Abū Bakr ibn Abi Maryam told me from the elders, that the Prophet ﷺ said:

"*Indeed, Allah, the Almighty, descends to the lowest heaven on the afternoon of 'Arafah, then He turns to His angels and says:*

'*Behold, each delegation has a reward, and these are My delegation, coming to Me disheveled and dusty. Grant them what they ask for, and compensate them for what they have spent.*'

Then, when the sun sets, He turns to them and says:

'*Behold, I have forgiven your wrongdoers for your righteous, and granted your righteous what they asked for. Depart in the name of Allah*'.*"

Ibrāhīm ibn al-Ḥakam ibn Abān narrated: My father told us, Farqad told us, that the gates of Heaven are opened three times every night, seven times on the night of Friday, and nine times on the night of 'Arafah.

We narrated from the transmission of Nufay' Abū Dāwūd, from Ibn 'Umar, both *marfū'* and *mawqūf*:

"*On the afternoon of the Day of 'Arafah, no one with even a mustard seed's weight of faith in his heart remains without being forgiven.*"

He was asked, "Is this forgiveness for those who are at the *wuqūf* (standing place at 'Arafah) specifically, or for people in general?"

He replied, "Nay, rather, it is for people in general."

---

[1] Attributed in '*Kanz al-'Ummāl*' (12103) to Ibn 'Asākir from Anas ﷺ.

Imām Mālik reported in 'Al-Muwaṭṭa' from the *mursal* narrations of Ṭalḥah ibn 'Ubaydillāh ibn Khariz that the Prophet ﷺ, said:

« مَا رُئِيَ الشَّيْطَانُ يَوْمًا هُوَ فِيهِ أَصْغَرُ ، وَلَا أَدْحَرُ وَلَا أَحْقَرُ ، وَلَا أَغْيَظُ مِنْهُ فِي يَوْمِ عَرَفَة ؛ وَمَا ذَاكَ إِلَّا لِمَا رَأَى مِن تَنَزُّلِ الرَّحْمَةِ ، وَتَجَاوُزِ اللهِ عَنِ الذُّنُوبِ العِظَامِ ، إِلَّا مَا أُرِيَ يَوْمَ بَدْرٍ » .

قِيل : وما رأى يوم بدر؟ قال : « رَأَى جِبْرِيلَ وَهُوَ يَزَعُ المَلَائِكَة »

"*Satan is not seen on any day smaller, more defeated, more humiliated, or more enraged than on the Day of Arafah. This is due to the mercy descending and Allah's forgiveness of great sins on that day; except what he saw on the day of Badr.*"

It was asked, "What did he see on the day of Badr?"

He said, "*he saw Gabriel organising the angels.*" [1]

A DAY OF DESPONDENCY & HUMILIATION FOR SATAN

Abū 'Uthmān al-Ṣābūnī narrated with his chain of transmission from a man who was a captive in the land of the Romans, and he escaped from one of the fortresses. He said:

"I used to travel by night and hide by day. One night, as I was walking between mountains and trees, I heard a noise that frightened me. I looked and saw a man riding a camel. I became even more terrified because there are no camels in the land of the Romans. I said:

"Glory be to Allah! In the land of the Romans, a man riding a camel? This is truly strange." When he reached me, I said:

"O servant of Allah, who are you?" He said, "Do not ask." I said, "I see something strange, so tell me." He said:

---

[1] Reported by Mālik in 'Al-Muwaṭṭa' (272) as *mursal*.

"Do not ask." But I insisted, and he said, "I am Iblis, and I have come from 'Arafāt. I was there this afternoon, looking at them. Mercy and forgiveness descended upon them, and they were granted pardon. This caused me distress, sorrow, and sadness. Now, I am heading to Constantinople to find relief in hearing the association of partners with Allah and the claim that He has a son."

I said, "I seek refuge in Allah from you." When I said these words, I saw no one.

This story is supported by the *ḥadīth* of 'Abbās ibn Mirdās, reported by Aḥmad and Ibn Mājah, about the Prophet's ﷺ supplication for his *ummah* on the afternoon of 'Arafah, and then at Muzdalifah.

It was answered, and the Prophet ﷺ laughed and said:

« إِنَّ إِبْلِيسَ حِينَ عَلِمَ أَنَّ اللهَ قَدْ غَفَرَ لِأُمَّتِي وَاسْتَجَابَ دُعَائِي أَهوى يُحْثِي التُّرَابَ عَلَى رَأْسِهِ ، وَيَدْعُو بِالوَيْلِ وَالثّبُورِ ؛ فَضَحِكْتُ مِنَ الْخَبِيثِ مِنْ جَزْعِهِ »

When Iblīs knew that Allah had forgiven my ummah and answered my supplication, he threw dust on his head and cried out in woe and despair. I laughed at the wretched one's distress. [1]

It is narrated from 'Alī bin al-Muwaffaq that he stood in 'Arafāt during one of his pilgrimages and saw the large number of people. He said:

"O Allah, if You have not accepted from anyone here, then accept my Ḥajj as a gift for them."

He saw the Glorified Lord in his dream, who said to him:

"O Ibn al-Muwaffaq! Are you being generous with Me? I have forgiven the people of the standing and their like, and I have granted each one of them intercession for their family, descendants, and tribe. I am the One worthy of piety and forgiveness."

Similar narrations are also reported from other sheikhs.

---

[1] Reported by Aḥmad (4/14), Ibn Mājah (3013), and Abū Dawūd (5234) in a summarised form.

ATTAINING FORGIVENESS & DELIVERANCE FROM HELLFIRE ON THE DAY OF 'ARAFAH

Therefore, whoever hopes for deliverance from Hellfire and the forgiveness of his sins on the Day of 'Arafah should adhere to the means that are hoped to achieve deliverance and forgiveness:

❖ One of them is **fasting on that day**.

THE FAST OF THE DAY OF 'ARAFAH

In '*Ṣaḥīḥ Muslim*', it is narrated from Abū Qatādah ﷺ that the Prophet ﷺ said:

« صِيَامُ يَوْمِ عَرَفَة ؛ أَحْتَسِبُ عَلَى الله أَنْ يُكَفِّرَ السَّنَةَ الَّتِي قَبْلَهُ وَالَّتِي بَعْدَه »

*Fasting on the Day of 'Arafah; I hope from Allah that it will expiate
the sins of the year before and the year after.* [1]

❖ Another is **guarding one's limbs from prohibited actions** on that day.

In the '*Musnad*' of Imām Aḥmad, it is narrated from Ibn 'Abbās ﷺ that the Prophet ﷺ said:

« يَوْمُ عَرَفَة ، هَذَا يَوْمٌ مَنْ مَلَكَ فِيهِ سَمْعَهُ وَبَصَرَهُ وَلِسَانَهُ ، غُفِرَ لَهُ »

*The Day of 'Arafah is a day when whoever controls his
hearing, sight, and tongue will be forgiven.* [2]

---

[1] Reported by Muslim (1162) and Abū Dāwūd (2425).
[2] Reported by Aḥmad (1/329), Ibn Khuzaymah (2832).

❖ Another is to **frequently recite the testimony of *Tawḥīd* with sincerity and truthfulness,** as it is the foundation of Islam, which Allah perfected on that day, and its basis.

THE BEST DHIKR FOR THE DAY OF 'ARAFAH

In 'Al-Musnad', it is narrated from 'Abdullāh ibn 'Amr ﷺ, who said: The most frequent supplication of the Prophet ﷺ on the Day of 'Arafah was:

لَا إِلٰهَ إِلَّا اللهُ وَحْدَهُ لَا شَرِيكَ لَهُ ۞ لَهُ الْمُلْكُ ۞ وَلَهُ الْحَمْدُ ۞

بِيَدِهِ الْخَيْرُ ۞ وَهُوَ عَلٰى كُلِّ شَيْءٍ قَدِيرٌ ۞

[*Lā ilāha illa-llāhu waḥdahu lā sharīka lahu, Lahu-l Mulku, Wa lahu-l ḥamdu,*
Biyadihi-l khayr, Wa huwa 'alā kulli shay'in qadīr]

There is no god but Allah alone, He has no partner, His is the dominion,
His is the praise, in His Hand is all good, and He is capable of all things.

Tirmidhī reported it with the wording:

« خَيْرُ الدُّعَاءِ دُعَاءُ يَوْمِ عَرَفَةَ ، وَخَيْرُ مَا قُلْتُ – أَنَا وَالنَّبِيُّونَ مِنْ قَبْلِي –:

لَا إِلَهَ إِلَّا اللهُ وَحْدَهُ لَا شَرِيكَ لَهُ ، لَهُ الْمُلْكُ وَلَهُ الْحَمْدُ ، وَهُوَ عَلَى كُلِّ شَيْءٍ قَدِيرٌ »

The best supplication is the supplication on the Day of 'Arafah,
and the best of what I and the Prophets before me have said is:

لَا إِلٰهَ إِلَّا اللهُ وَحْدَهُ لَا شَرِيكَ لَهُ ۞ لَهُ الْمُلْكُ وَلَهُ الْحَمْدُ ۞

وَهُوَ عَلٰى كُلِّ شَيْءٍ قَدِيرٌ ۞

[*Lā ilāha illa-llāhu waḥdahu lā sharīka lahu,*
Lahu-l Mulku wa lahu-l ḥamdu, Wa huwa 'alā kulli shay'in qadīr]

*There is no god but Allah alone, He has no partner, His is the dominion
and His is the praise, and He is capable of all things.* [1]

Ṭabarānī also reported it as *marfūʿ* from the *ḥadīth* of ʿAlī and
Ibn ʿUmar. [2]

Imām Aḥmad reported from the *ḥadīth* of Al-Zubayr ibn Al-
ʿAwwām, who said: I heard the Messenger of Allah ﷺ, while he was at
ʿArafah, reciting this verse:

﴿ شَهِدَ اللهُ أَنَّهُ لَا إِلَهَ إِلَّا هُوَ وَالْمَلَٰئِكَةُ وَأُولُوا الْعِلْمِ ﴾

*Allah, the angels and those of knowledge bear witness
that there is no deity except Him*
[Āl ʿImrān : 18]

and saying:

« وأنا على ذلك من الشاهدين، يا رب »

And I am among the witnesses, O Lord. [3]

It is also narrated from the *ḥadīth* of ʿUbādah ibn al-Ṣāmit ﷺ,
who said: "I witnessed the Prophet ﷺ on the Day of ʿArafah, and the
most frequent thing he said was:

﴿ شَهِدَ اللهُ أَنَّهُ لَا إِلَهَ إِلَّا هُوَ ﴾

Then he said: "*O Lord, and I bear witness.*"

Fulfilling the word of *Tawḥīd* necessitates deliverance from
Hellfire, as it is equivalent to freeing slaves, and freeing slaves results
in deliverance from the fire.

As it is established in the authentic traditions that whoever
says it one hundred times, it is equivalent to freeing ten slaves.

---

[1] Reported by Aḥmad (2/210) and Tirmidhī (3585).
[2] Reported by Ṭabarānī in 'al-Duʿā' (874) from ʿAlī, and from Ibn ʿUmar (875).
[3] Reported by Aḥmad (1/166). Haythamī said in 'Majmaʿ al-Zawāʾid' (6/325): "It was narrated by
Aḥmad and Ṭabarānī, and in their chains are unknown narrators."

It is also established that whoever says it ten times, it is as if he freed four of the descendants of Ismā'īl ﷺ.[1]

In '*Sunan Abī Dāwūd*' and others, from Anas ﷺ, from the Prophet ﷺ, who said: *"Whoever says in the morning or evening:*

اَللَّهُمَّ إِنِّى أَصْبَحْتُ أُشْهِدُكَ وَأُشْهِدُ حَمْلَةَ عَرْشِكَ وَمَلَائِكَتَكَ وَجَمِيعَ خَلْقِكَ

أَنَّكَ أَنْتَ اللَّهُ لَا إِلَهَ إِلَّا أَنْتَ وَأَنَّ مُحَمَّدًا عَبْدُكَ وَرَسُولُكَ

'O Allah, I have become a witness to You, the bearers of Your Throne, Your angels, and all of Your creation, that You are Allah, there is no deity except You, and Muhammad is Your servant and Messenger,'

Allah will free one-fourth of him from the fire. Whoever says it twice, Allah will free half of him from the fire. Whoever says it three times, Allah will free three-quarters of him from the fire. Whoever says it four times, Allah will free him from the fire."[2]

It is narrated from the *mursal* reports of Zuhrī: "Whoever says

لَا إِلَهَ إِلَّا اللَّهُ وَحْدَهُ لَا شَرِيكَ لَهُ ۞

ten thousand times in one day, Allah will free him from the fire."

Just as if he brought a ransom of ten thousand for someone he killed, it would be accepted from him.

FREEDOM & SALVATION

❖ Another means is **to free a slave if possible**; for whoever frees a believing slave, Allah will free every limb of him from the fire in return for every limb of the slave.

---

[1] Reported by Bukhārī (6404), Muslim (2693), Aḥmad (5/418), and Tirmidhī (3553).
[2] Reported by Abū Dāwūd (5069).

Ḥakīm bin Ḥizām ﷺ, used to stand at ‘Arafah with one hundred camels adorned with garlands and one hundred slaves, and he would free his slaves.

The people would cry and supplicate, saying: "Our Lord, this is Your servant who has freed his slaves, and we are Your servants, so free us."

Once, a similar event happened with the people and Al-Rashīd.

Abū Qilābah used to free a slave girl on *‘Īd al-Fiṭr*, hoping that Allah would free him from the fire because of that.

❖ Another means is to **frequently supplicate for forgiveness and deliverance from the fire**, as it is hoped that supplication will be answered on that day.

Ibn Abī Dunyā narrated with his chain from ‘Alī, who said: "There is no day on earth except that Allah frees slaves from the fire, and there is no day on which more slaves are freed than the Day of ‘Arafah."

So, increase in saying on that day:

اَللّٰهُمَّ أَعْتِقْ رَقَبَتِي مِنَ النَّارِ ❁ وَأَوْسِعْ لِي مِنَ الرِّزْقِ الْحَلَالِ ❁ وَاصْرِفْ عَنِّي فَسَقَةَ الْجِنِّ وَالْإِنْسِ

O Allah, free my neck from the fire, expand for me lawful provision, and turn away from me the wicked among jinn and humans.

For this is generally my supplication on this (blessed) day (of ‘Arafah).

فَنَفْسَكَ لُمْ وَلَا تَلِم الْمَطَايَا وَمُتْ كمدا فَلَيْسَ لَكَ اعْتِذَارُ

Blame yourself, do not blame the mounts ...

Die of sorrow, for you have no excuse

If you hope for deliverance, then **buy yourself from Allah**, for

﴿ إِنَّ اللّٰهَ اشْتَرَى مِنَ الْمُؤْمِنِينَ أَنْفُسَهُمْ وَأَمْوَالَهُمْ بِأَنَّ لَهُمُ الْجَنَّةَ ﴾

Allah certainly has purchased from the believers their souls and their wealth in exchange that there is Paradise for them [Al-Tawbah : 111]

Whoever values his soul will find it easy to give up anything to save it from the Fire.

Some of the predecessors bought themselves from Allah three or four times, each time giving charity equivalent to their weight in silver.

Amer ibn ‘Abdillāh ibn Az-Zubayr bought himself from Allah with his blood-money six times, giving it in charity.

Ḥabīb Al-‘Ajamī bought himself from Allah with forty thousand dirhams, giving them in charity.

Abū Hurayrah ﷺ used to glorify Allah twelve thousand times a day, equal to his blood-money, thereby freeing himself.

فَمَنِ الَّذِى يَبْـــــــتَاعُ بِالثَّمَنِ   بِدَمِ الْمُحِبّ يُـــــــبَاعُ وَصْلُهُمْ

With the blood of the lover, their connection is sold ...
So who will buy with the price?

Whoever knows what they seek will find it easy to give up anything.

Woe to you! We have accepted your regret for freeing yourself, and we are content with your repentance and sorrow as the price.

During this season, the price has been reduced; whoever controls his hearing, sight, and tongue will be forgiven.

Extend your hand in apology, stand at His door with humility and brokenness, raise the story of your regret, written on the tablet of your cheek with the ink of flowing tears, and say:

﴿ رَبَّنَا ظَلَمْنَآ أَنْفُسَنَا سكتة وَإِنْ لَّمْ تَغْفِرْ لَنَا وَتَرْحَمْنَا لَنَكُوْنَنَّ مِنَ الْخُسِرِيْنَ ﴾

O our Lord, we wronged ourselves, and if You do not forgive us and show mercy
upon us, we will most certainly be among the losing ones.
[Al-A‘rāf : 23]

Yaḥyā ibn Mu‘ādh said: The servant alienates himself from his Master with disobedience, but he never leaves His door under any circumstances; knowing that the honour of the servant is in the shadow of their Master.

Then he recited:

قُرَّةُ عَيْنِي لَا بُدَّ لِي مِنْكَ وَإِنْ   أَوحشَ بَيْنِي وَبَيْـــــــنَكَ الزَّلَلُ

قُرَّةُ عَيْنِي أَنَا الْغَـــــــرِيقُ فَخُذْ   كَفَّ غَرِيقٍ عَلَيْكَ يَتَّـــــــكِلُ

Delight of my eyes, I cannot do without you even if...
        Sins have alienated me from you
Delight of my eyes, I am drowning, so take ...
        The hand of a drowning one who relies on you

The states of the truthful at the standing in 'Arafah varied. Some were overwhelmed by fear and some by shame.

Muṭarrif ibn 'Abdillāh ibn Al-Shakhīr and Bakr Al-Muzanī stood at 'Arafah, and one of them said:

"O Allah, do not turn away the people of the standing because of me."

The other said: "What an honourable and hopeful position it is for its people, if only I were not among them!"

Fuḍayl stood at 'Arafah while people were supplicating, and he was weeping like a bereaved mother, crying so much that it prevented him from making supplication.

When the sun was about to set, he raised his head to the sky and said:

وا سوءتاه منك وإن عفوت!

"Oh, what a disgrace from You, even if You forgive!"

Fuḍayl also said to Shu'ayb ibn Ḥarb during the pilgrimage: "If you think that anyone at the standing place is worse than you and me, then what a bad thought you have."

One of the knowledgeable ones prayed at 'Arafah, saying: "O Allah, if You did not accept my Ḥajj, my effort, and my hardship, do not deprive me of the reward for the calamity of Your refusal to accept from me."

One of the fearful ones stood at 'Arafah until the sun was about to set, then he cried out: "Safety! Safety! The departure is near! I wish I knew what You did with the needs of the poor!"

أَرَى الْمَوْتَ وَالْعَيْشَ فِيْكُمْ عَيَانَا   وَإِنِّي مِنْ خَـــوْفِكُمْ وَالرَّجَا

أَتَاكُمْ يُنَادِى الْأَمَـــانَ الْأَمَانَا   فَمُنُّوا عَلَى تَـــائِبٍ خَائِفٍ

Indeed, from fear of You and hope …
> *I see death and life with You clearly*

So bestow upon a repentant, fearful one …
> *Who has come to You, crying out for safety, safety*

When a captive asks for safety from the noble king, he grants it.

وَذُنُوبِي إِذَا عَدَدَنْ تَطُـــولُ   الْأَمَانَ الْأَمَانَ وِزْرِى ثَقِـــيلُ

فَتَرَى لِي إِلَى الْخَلَاصِ سَبِـــيلُ؟   أَوبَقَتْنِي وَأَوْثَقَـــتْنِي ذُنُـــوبِي

Safety, safety, my burden is heavy …
> *And my sins, if counted, are many*

My sins have ruined me and bound me …
> *Do You see for me a way to salvation?*

One of the fearful knowledgeable ones stood at 'Arafah, and his shyness prevented him from supplicating.

He was asked: "Why do you not supplicate?" He replied: "There is estrangement."

He was told: "This is the day of forgiveness of sins," so he raised his hands and fell dead.

فَاسْتَذْكَرَتْ عَهْدًا لَهَا بِالْبَـــانِ   حدا بِهَا الْحَادِى إِلَى نُعْمَـــانِ

تَشَوُّقًا إِلَى الزَّمَانِ الْفَـــانِي   فَسَالَتِ الرُّوحُ مِنَ الْأَجْفَـــانِ

The guide led them to Nu'mān ...
So she remembered a covenant with the Ban trees
The soul flowed from the eyelids ...
Longing for the passing time

Another poet says:

قَدْ جَنَّ بِهِمْ وَهَكَذَا الْبَلْبَـــــــالُ   قَدْ لَجَّ بِي الْغَرَامُ حَتَّى قَـــــــالُوا

فِي مِثْلِ هَوَاكَ تَرْخُص الْأَجَـــــــالُ   الْمَوْتُ إِذَا رَضِـــــيتَه سِلْسَـــــالُ

Passion has overwhelmed me until they said ...
They have gone mad, and so is the yearning
Death, if accepted, is a chain ...
In love like yours, lives are cheapened

One of the fearful ones stood at 'Arafāt and said: "My Lord, people are drawing near to You with sacrifices, and I am drawing near to You with myself;" then he fell dead.

تُهْدِى الْأَضَاحِى وَأُهْدِى مُهْجَتِي وَدَمِي   لِلنَّاسِ حَجٌّ وَلِي حَجٌّ إِلَى سَـــــكَنِي

People perform Ḥajj, and my Ḥajj is to my dwelling ...
They offer sacrifices, and I offer my soul and blood

Lovers are not satisfied for their beloved with the shedding of the blood of sacrifices; rather, they offer their souls.

وَمَا الْعِيدُ عِنْدِى غَيْرَ قُرْبَ الْحَبَائِبِ   أَرَى مَوْسِمَ الْأَعْيَادِ أُنَسَ الْأَجَـــــانِبِ

فَإِنْ قَبِلُوا قَلْبِي وَإِلَّا فَقَـــــالِبِي   إِذَا قَرَّبُوا بِدنًا فَقُرْبَانِي الْهَـــــوَى

وَلَكِنْ بِمَا بَيْنَ الْحَشَا وَالتَّرَائِبِ   وَمَا بِدَمِ الْأَنْعَامِ أَقْضَى حُقُوقَهُمْ

I see the season of festivities as the joy of strangers ...
But for me, 'Īd is nothing but the closeness of loved ones
If they offer sacrificial animals, my offering is love ...
If they accept my heart, otherwise, my body

I do not fulfill their rights with the blood of animals ...
But with what is between the heart and ribs

Abū 'Ubaydah Al-Khawwāṣ was overwhelmed with longing and anxiety to the point that he would beat his chest on the road, saying: "Oh, my longing for the One who sees me, but I do not see Him."

After he grew older, he would hold his beard and say: "O Lord, I have grown old, so free me."

He was seen at 'Arafah, overcome with passionate longing, saying:

سُبْحَانَ مَنْ لَوْ سَجَدْنَا بِالْعُيُونِ لَهُ   عَلَى حِمَى الشَّوْكِ وَالْمَحْمَى مِنَ الْإِبرِ

لَمْ نَبْلُغِ الْعُشْرَ مِنْ معْشَارِ نِعْمَتِهِ   وَلَا الْعَشِيرَ وَلَا عَشَرًا مِّنَ الْعُشرِ

هُوَ الرَّفِيعُ فَلَا الْأَبْصَارُ تُدْرِكُهُ   سُبْحَانَهُ مَنْ مَلِيكٌ نَافِذُ الْقَدَرِ

سُبْحَانَ مَنْ هُوَ أُنِيي إِذْ خَلَوْتُ بِهِ   فِي جَوْفِ لَيْلِي وَفِي الظُّلُمَاتِ وَالسَّحَرِ

أَنْتَ الْحَبِيبُ وَأَنْتَ الْحُبُّ يَا أَمَلِي   مَنْ لِي سِوَاكَ وَمَنْ أَرْجُوهُ يَا ذخرِى

Glory be to the One, even if we prostrate with our eyes to Him ...
On thorny ground and heated needles
We would not reach a tenth of a tenth of His blessing ...
Nor a tenth of a tenth of a tenth
He is the Exalted, the sights do not perceive Him ...
Glory be to Him, the Sovereign of decisive decree
Glory be to the One who is my comfort when I am alone with Him ...
In the depth of my night, in darkness and in the early dawn
You are the Beloved, and You are love, O my hope ...
Who do I have but You, and whom do I hope for, O my treasure?

Among the knowledgeable ones, there are those who, in the moment of supplication, cling to the fringes of hope.

Ibn al-Mubārak said: I came to Sufyān al-Thawrī on the eve of 'Arafah, and he was kneeling on his knees with tears streaming from his eyes.

He turned to me, and I asked him, "Who is in the worst state among this gathering?"

He replied, "The one who thinks that Allah will not forgive them."

It is narrated from Fuḍayl that he looked at the people's sobbing and weeping on the eve of 'Arafah and said:

"Do you see if these people went to a man and asked him for a small coin, meaning one-sixth of a dirham, would he refuse them?"

They replied, "No."

He said: "By Allah, forgiveness from Allah is easier than a man's response to them with a small coin."

وَأَعْلَمُ أَنَّ اللَّهَ يَعْفُو وَيَغْفِـــرُ   وَإِنِّي لَأَدْعُو اللَّهَ أَسْأَلُ عَفْــــوَهُ

وَإِنْ عَظُمَتْ فِي رَحْمَةِ اللَّهِ تُصْـــغَرُ   لَئِنْ أَعْظَمَ النَّاسُ الذُّنُـــوبَ فَإِنَّهَا

Indeed, I supplicate to Allah asking for His pardon ...
And I know that Allah forgives and pardons
Even if people's sins are great ...
They become small in the mercy of Allah

A NON-PILGRIM IN THE SEASON OF HAJJ

In a little while, your brothers will stand at 'Arafah in that position, so congratulations to those who are granted it!

They cry out to Allah with burning hearts and flowing tears; among them are those frightened by fear, and it disturbed them, and lovers ignited by longing, and it burned them, and hopeful ones who trusted in Allah's promise and believed it, and repentants who sincerely repented to Allah and were truthful, and fugitives who sought refuge at Allah's door and knocked on it.

How many there are who deserved Hellfire but Allah saved and freed them, and prisoners of sins whom He released and freed.

Then the most Merciful of the merciful looks upon them, boasts about them to the inhabitants of the heavens, draws near and says:

"What do these want? We have cut off deprivation at their arrival and given them the ultimate of their desires. He is the one who gives and withholds, connects and severs."

مَا أَصْنَعُ هَكَذَا جَرَى الْمَقْـــــــــدُورُ   الْجَبْرُ لِغَيْرِى وَأَنَا الْمَكْسُـــــــورُ

أَسِيرُ ذَنْبٍ مُقَيَّدٌ مَا ســـــــــــور   هَلْ يُمْكِنُ أَن يُّبَدَّلَ الْمَسْـــــــطُورُ

What can I do? Thus is the decree ...
        Mending is for others, and I am the broken one
A prisoner of sin, bound and constrained ...
        Can what is written be changed?

Whoever missed standing at ʿArafah this year, let him stand for Allah with the right He knows.

Whoever is unable to spend the night at Muzdalifah, let him resolve to obey Allah, for He has brought him near and made him close.

Whoever cannot perform the acts at Al-Khayf, let him stand for Allah with the right of hope and fear.

Whoever cannot sacrifice his offering at Minā, let him slaughter his desires here, for he has reached the goal.

Whoever cannot reach the House because it is far from him, let him intend the Lord of the House; for He is closer to the one who calls upon Him and hopes for Him than the jugular vein.

In these days, a breath of intimacy from the gardens of sanctity has blown upon every heart that responded to what it was called to.

O ambitions of the knowers! Do not be content with anything but Allah!

O determinations of the worshipers! Gather for all the devotions of the seekers!

Devote yourself to the love of your Master, and unite between His fear and hope, and enjoy His remembrance.

O secrets of the lovers! Circumambulate and bow at the Ka'bah of love; strive and hasten between the clarity of Ṣafā and the sincerity of Marwah.

Stand and supplicate at the 'Arafāt of knowledge, then proceed to the nearness of Muzdalifah, and then return to Minā for the attainment of desires.

When the sacrifices are brought, offer your souls and do not withhold; the path has become clear today, but the sincere travellers are few and the claimants are many.

لَئِن لَمْ أَحُجَّ الْبَيْتَ إِذْ شَطَّ رَبْعَهُ   حَجَجْتُ إِلَى مَن لَّا يَغِيبُ عَنِ الذِّكْرِ

فَأَحْرَمْتُ مِن وَقْتِي بِخَلْعِ نَقَائِصِى   أَطُوفُ وَأَسْعَى فِي اللَّطَائِفِ وَالْبِرِّ

صَفَائَ صَفَائِى عَنْ صِفَاتِى وَمَرْوَتِى   مَرُوءَةُ قَلْبٍ عَنْ سِوَى حُبِّهِ قفر

وَفِي عَرَفَاتِ الْأُنْسِ بِاللَّهِ مَوْقِفِى   وَمُزْدَلِفِى الزُّلْفَى لَدَيْهِ إِلَى الْحَشَرِ

وَبِـــــــتُّ الْمُنَى مِنِّى   مَبِـــــــيتِى فِي مِنًى

وَرَمْىُ جَمَـــــــارِى جَمْرُ شَوْقٍ فِي صَـــــدْرِى

وَإِشْعَارُ هَدْيِى ذَبْحُ نَفْسِى بِقَهْرِهَا   وَحَلْقِى بِمَحْقِ الْكَائِنَاتِ عَنِ الْبِرِّ

وَمَنْ رَامَ نَفْرًا بَعْدَ نُسْكِ فَإِنَّنِى   مُقِيمٌ عَلَى نُسْكِى حَيَاتِى بِلَا نَفْرِ

Even if I did not perform Ḥajj to the House because its location is far …
I performed Ḥajj to the One who is never absent from remembrance
I entered the state of Ihram by shedding my faults …
I circumambulate and strive in kindness and goodness

My Safa is my purification from my traits, and my Marwa ...
          Is the chivalry of a heart devoid of anything but His love
And at the Arafat of intimacy with Allah is my standing ...
          And my Muzdalifah is my approaching Him until the resurrection
I fulfilled my hopes ...
          By spending the night in Minā

And casting my pebbles is the embers of my longing in my chest

And marking my sacrifice is the slaughter of my soul by subduing it ...
          And my shaving is the annihilation of creatures from the secret
Whoever seeks departure after rituals, I ...
          Remain on my rituals throughout my life without departure

AL-MAJLIS AL-THĀLITH:
THE DAYS OF TASHRĪQ

Muslim recorded in his 'Ṣaḥīḥ' from the ḥadīth of Nubayshah al-Hudhalī ﷺ that the Prophet ﷺ said:

« أَيَّامُ مِنَى أَيَّامُ أَكْلٍ وَشُرْبٍ ، وَذِكْرِ الله ﷻ »

*The days of Minā are days of eating, drinking,
and remembrance of Allah the Exalted.* [1]

THE APPOINTED DAYS OF FESTIVITY & DHIKR

The scholars of the *Sunan* and *Masānīd* recorded it through various chains from the Prophet ﷺ; in some of them, the Prophet ﷺ sent a caller during the days of Minā, proclaiming:

« لَا تَصُومُوا هَذِهِ الأَيَّامِ ؛ فَإِنَّهَا أَيَّامُ أَكْلٍ وَشُرْبٍ وَذِكْرِ الله ﷻ »

---

[1] Reported by Muslim (1142), Aḥmad (76, 5/75), Abū Dawūd (2830, 2813), Nasā'ī (7/170), and Ibn Mājah (3167, 3160).

*Do not fast on these days; they are days of eating, drinking,
and remembrance of Allah the Exalted.* [1]

In a narration by Nasā'ī:

« أَيَّامُ أَكْلٍ وَشُرْبٍ وَصَلَاةٍ »

They are days of eating, drinking, and prayer. [2]

In a narration by Dāraquṭnī - with a weak chain -:

« أَيَّامُ أَكْلٍ وَشُرْبٍ وَبَعَالٍ »

They are days of eating, drinking, and intimacy. [3]

In a narration by Imām Aḥmad:

« مَن كَانَ صَائِمًا فَلْيُفْطِرْ ؛ فَإِنَّهَا أَيَّامُ أَكْلٍ وَشُرْبٍ »

*Whoever is fasting, let him break his fast;
for they are days of eating and drinking.* [4]

In another narration:

« إِنَّهَا لَيْسَتْ أَيَّامُ صِيَامٍ »

They are not days of fasting. [5]

The days of Minā are the appointed days mentioned by Allah the
Exalted in His words:

﴿ وَاذْكُرُوا اللَّهَ فِي أَيَّامٍ مَّعْدُودَاتٍ ﴾

And remember Allah in the appointed days
[Al-Baqarah : 203]

---

[1] Reported by Aḥmad (3/494) from Ḥamzah ibn 'Amr Al-Aslamī ﷺ.
[2] Reported by Nasā'ī in '*Al-Kubrā*' (2914) from the *ḥadīth* of 'Abdullāh ibn 'Amr.
[3] Reported by Dāraquṭnī in '*Sunan*' (2/212) with Wāqidī in its chain, and Dāraquṭnī said after narrating this *ḥadīth*: Wāqidī is weak.
[4] Reported by Aḥmad (5/224) from a companion of the Prophet ﷺ.
[5] Refer to '*Majma' Al-Zawā'id*' (3/202-203).

THE APPOINTED DAYS IN HAJJ

These are three days after the Day of *Naḥr* (sacrifice), and they are the Days of *Tashrīq*. This is the opinion of Ibn 'Umar and most scholars.

It is also narrated from Ibn 'Abbās ﷺ and 'Aṭā' ﷺ that they are four days: the Day of *Naḥr* and the three days after it; and 'Aṭā' called them the Days of *Tashrīq*.

The first opinion is more apparent.

The Prophet ﷺ said:

« أَيَّامُ مِنَى ثَلَاثَة : ﴿ فَمَنْ تَعَجَّلَ فِي يَوْمَيْنِ فَلَآ اِثْمَ عَلَيْهِ وَمَنْ تَأَخَّرَ فَلَآ اِثْمَ عَلَيْهِ ﴾ »

The days of Minā are three: { So whoever hastens in two days there is no sin upon him; and whoever delays there is no sin upon him [Al-Baqarah : 203] }.

The scholars of the four *Sunan* narrated this from the *ḥadīth* of 'Abd al-Raḥmān ibn Ya'mar, from the Prophet ﷺ. [1]

This is explicit in that they are the days of *Tashrīq*.

The best of them is the first, which is the Day of Settlement (*Yawm Al-Qarr*), because the people of Minā settle in it, and it is not permissible to depart.

In the ḥadīth of 'Abdullāh ibn Qurṭ from the Prophet ﷺ:

« أَعْظَمُ الأَيَّام عِنْدَ الله يَوْمَ النَّحْرِ ، ثُمَّ يَوْمَ القَرِّ »

The greatest days before Allah are the Day of Sacrifice,
then the Day of Settlement.

It is narrated from Sa'īd ibn Al-Musayyib that the Greatest Day of Ḥajj is the Day of Settlement, which is a (ḥadīth) *gharīb*.

---

[1] Reported by Aḥmad (335, 310, 4/309), Abū Dawūd (1949), Tirmidhī (890, 889), Nasā'ī (264, 5/256), and Ibn Mājah (3015).

A part of the ḥadīth states: « الحج عرفة ... » *"Ḥajj is Arafah..."* and it is an authentic *ḥadīth*.

Then comes the first day of departure (*Yawm al-Nafr al-Awwal*), which is the middle one, followed by the second day of departure (*Yawm al-Nafr al-Thānī*), which is the last one.

Allah the Exalted said:

﴿ فَمَنْ تَعَجَّلَ فِي يَوْمَيْنِ فَلَا إِثْمَ عَلَيْهِ ۚ وَمَنْ تَأَخَّرَ فَلَا إِثْمَ عَلَيْهِ ﴾

So whoever hastens in two days there is no sin upon him;
and whoever delays there is no sin upon him
[Al-Baqarah : 203]

Many of the predecessors said: This means that the one who hastens and the one who delays are both forgiven, and their sins are removed, if they performed Ḥajj without obscenity or disobedience, and they return free from sins as on the day their mother bore them. For this reason, Allah the Exalted said:

﴿ لِمَنِ اتَّقَىٰ ﴾

For whoever is conscious of Allah.
[Al-Baqarah : 203]

Thus, piety becomes a condition for the removal of sin according to this interpretation, and the verse indicates what the Prophet ﷺ explicitly stated:

« مَنْ حَجَّ فَلَمْ يَرْفُثْ وَلَمْ يَفْسُقْ رَجَعَ مِن ذُنُوبِهِ كَيَوْمِ وَلَدَتْهُ أُمُّهُ »

Whoever performs Ḥajj and does not engage in obscenity or disobedience will return (free of sin) as on the day his mother bore him. [1]

---

[1] Reported by Bukhārī (1521, 1819), Muslim (108, 1350), Aḥmad (494, 484, 410, 2/248), Tirmidhī (811), Nasā'ī (114/5), and Ibn Mājah (2889) from the *ḥadīth* of Abū Hurayrah ﷺ.

DHIKR OF ALLAH IN THE APPOINTED DAYS

Allah the Exalted commanded the remembrance of Him during these appointed days, as the Prophet ﷺ said:

$$\text{« إِنَّهَا أَيَّامُ أَكْلٍ وَشُرْبٍ وَذِكْرِ الله ﷺ »}$$

They are days of eating, drinking, and remembrance of Allah the Exalted.

The remembrance of Allah, the Exalted, which is commanded during the days of *Tashrīq* includes various types:

❖ One of them is the remembrance of Allah, the Exalted, **following the obligatory prayers by saying the *takbīr* after them.**

This is prescribed until the end of the days of *Tashrīq* according to the majority of scholars.

It has been narrated from 'Umar, 'Alī, and Ibn 'Abbās. There is a *ḥadīth* raised through ascription on this, although with a weak chain.

❖ Another is the *dhikr* of Allah by mentioning His name and saying the *takbīr* **when slaughtering the sacrificial animals.**

The time for slaughtering the sacrificial animals extends to the end of the days of *Tashrīq* according to a group of scholars, which is the opinion of Shāfi'ī and a narration from Imām Aḥmad . There is a *marfū'* *ḥadīth* on this: *"All the days of Minā are for slaughtering."* [1] Its chain has some discussion.

Most of the Companions ﷺ hold that the slaughtering is specific to the two days of *Tashrīq* along with the Day of *Naḥr*.

---

[1] Reported by Aḥmad (4/82).

This is the famous opinion of Aḥmad, and also the opinion of Mālik, Abū Ḥanīfah, and the majority.

❖   Another is the *dhikr* of Allah **during eating and drinking**.

It is prescribed to mention Allah's name at the beginning of eating and to praise Him at the end.

In the *ḥadīth* from the Prophet ﷺ:

« إنَّ اللهَ ﷻ يَرْضَى عَنِ العَبْدِ أَنْ يَأْكُلَ الأَكْلَةَ فَيَحْمَدَهُ عَلَيْهَا ،

وَيَشْرَبَ الشَّرْبَةَ فَيَحْمَدَهُ عَلَيْهَا »

Indeed, Allah is pleased with the servant who eats a meal and praises Him for it, and drinks a drink and praises Him for it. [1]

It has been narrated that whoever mentions Allah's name at the beginning of his food and praises Allah at the end has paid its price and will not be asked further about his gratitude.

❖   Another is the *dhikr* of Allah by saying the *takbīr* **when throwing the pebbles** during the days of *Tashrīq*,

This is specific to the pilgrims.

❖   Another is **the general *dhikr* of Allah, the Exalted**;

It is recommended to increase in it during the days of *Tashrīq*.

'Umar used to say *takbīr* in Minā in his tent, and the people would hear him and say *takbīr*, causing Minā to resound with *takbīr*.

Allah the Exalted said:

﴿ فَإِذَا قَضَيْتُم مَّنَاسِكَكُمْ فَاذْكُرُوا اللَّهَ كَذِكْرِكُمْ آبَاءَكُمْ أَوْ أَشَدَّ ذِكْرًا ﴾

---

[1] Reported by Muslim (2734), and Tirmidhī (1816), from Anas ﷺ.

And when you have completed your rites, then remember Allah similar to your remembrance of your forefathers, or more intense remembrance.
[Al-Baqarah : 200].

﴿ فَمِنَ النَّاسِ مَنْ يَّقُوْلُ رَبَّنَآ اٰتِنَا فِي الدُّنْيَا وَمَا لَهُ فِي الْاٰخِرَةِ مِنْ خَلَاقٍ ۝

وَمِنْهُمْ مَّنْ يَّقُوْلُ رَبَّنَآ اٰتِنَا فِي الدُّنْيَا حَسَنَةً وَّفِي الْاٰخِرَةِ حَسَنَةً وَّقِنَا عَذَابَ النَّارِ ﴾

There are then those from among mankind who say: 'Our Lord, give us in this world,' and there is no share for him in the Hereafter. And there are those from among them who say, 'Our Lord, give us good in this world and good in the Hereafter, and protect us from the punishment of the Fire.'
[Al-Baqarah : 200-201]

Many of the pious predecessors recommended frequently making this supplication during the days of *Tashrīq*.

A RECOMMENDED SUNNAH DUʿĀ

'Ikrimah said: It was recommended to say during the days of *Tashrīq*:

رَبَّنَآ اٰتِنَا فِي الدُّنْيَا حَسَنَةً وَّفِي الْاٰخِرَةِ حَسَنَةً وَّقِنَا عَذَابَ النَّارِ

'Atā' said: It is proper for everyone who departs to say when heading to his family:

رَبَّنَآ اٰتِنَا فِي الدُّنْيَا حَسَنَةً وَّفِي الْاٰخِرَةِ حَسَنَةً وَّقِنَا عَذَابَ النَّارِ

This supplication is one of the most comprehensive supplications for goodness, and the Prophet ﷺ frequently made it.

It is narrated that it was his most frequent supplication;[1] whenever he made a supplication, he would include this, as it combines the goodness of this world and the Hereafter.

---

[1] Reported by Bukhārī (6389), and Muslim (2690), from the *ḥadīth* of Anas ﷺ with the wording:
كَانَ أَكْثَرُ دَعْوَةٍ يَدْعُو بِهَا رَسُولُ الله ﷺ : « اللَّهُمَّ رَبَّنَا آتِنَا فِي الدُّنْيَا حَسَنَةً ، وَفِي الآخِرَةِ حَسَنَةً ، وَقِنَا عَذَابَ النَّارِ »

Al-Ḥasan said: The good in this world is knowledge and worship, and in the Hereafter it is Paradise.

Sufyān said: The good in this world is knowledge and lawful provision, and in the Hereafter it is Paradise.

A TIME FOR DUʿĀ

Supplication is one of the best forms of the remembrance of Allah the Exalted.

Ziyād Al-Jaṣṣāṣ narrated from Abū Kinānah Al-Qurashī, that he heard Abū Mūsā Al-Ashʿarī ﷺ say in his sermon on the Day of *Naḥr*:

"After the Day of Sacrifice, there are three days which Allah mentioned as the appointed days. Supplication is not rejected during these days, so raise your desires to Allah the Exalted."

CONCLUDING ALL RITES WITH DHIKR

There is a meaning in the command to remember Allah at the conclusion of the rites, which is that all other acts of worship come to an end and are completed, but the remembrance of Allah remains and does not come to an end or completion; rather, it continues for the believers in this world and the Hereafter.

Allah the Exalted commanded His *dhikr* after the completion of prayer. Almighty Allah says:

$$\text{﴿ فَإِذَا قَضَيْتُمُ الصَّلٰوةَ فَاذْكُرُوا اللّٰهَ قِيَامًا وَّقُعُودًا وَّعَلٰى جُنُوْبِكُمْ ﴾}$$

Then when you complete the prayer, then remember Allah
standing, sitting, and [lying] on your sides. [An-Nisā' : 103]

"The most frequent supplication of the Prophet ﷺ was: 'O Allah, our Lord, give us in this world good, and in the Hereafter good, and protect us from the punishment of the Fire'."

Almighty Allah said about the Friday prayer:

﴿ فَإِذَا قُضِيَتِ الصَّلَوٰةُ فَانْتَشِرُوا فِي الْأَرْضِ وَابْتَغُوا مِنْ فَضْلِ اللهِ وَاذْكُرُوا اللهَ كَثِيرًا ﴾

Then when the prayer has been completed then disperse on the earth and
seek Allah's grace, and remember Allah abundantly
[Al-Jumu'ah: 10]

Allah the Exalted said:

﴿ فَإِذَا فَرَغْتَ فَانْصَبْ ۝ وَإِلَىٰ رَبِّكَ فَارْغَبْ ۝ ﴾

So when you have finished [your duties], then exert [in worship].
And to your Lord direct [your] longing.
[Ash-Sharḥ : 7-8]

It is narrated from Ibn Mas'ūd ﷺ, who said: When you have completed the obligatory duties, then stand up [for worship].

Also, about the words of Almighty Allah:

﴿ وَإِلَىٰ رَبِّكَ فَارْغَبْ ﴾

And to your Lord direct [your] longing
[Ash-Sharḥ : 8],

he (Ibn Mas'ūd ﷺ) said: In supplication, while you are sitting.

Al-Ḥasan said: Almighty Allah commanded him (ﷺ) that when he finishes from an expedition, he should strive in supplication and worship. All actions come to an end, but *dhikr* has no end or completion; actions cease with the end of the world, and nothing of them remains in the Hereafter, but *dhikr* does not cease. **The believer lives on *dhikr*, dies on it, and is resurrected on it.**

أَحَسِبْتُمْ أَنَّ اللَّيَالِيَ غَيَّرَتْ   عَهْدَ الْهَوَى لَا كَانَ مَنْ يَتَغَيَّرُ

يَفْنَى الزَّمَانُ وَلَيْسَ يفنى ذِكْرُكُمْ   وَعَلَى مَحَبَّتِكُمْ أَمُوتُ وَأُحْشَرُ

Did you think that the nights had changed ...
The covenant of love? No, may he never change
Time may perish, but your remembrance does not ...
And on your love, I will die and be resurrected

بِذِكْرِ اللهِ تَرْتَاحُ الْقُلُــــــــوبُ   وَدُنْيَانَا بِذِكْرَاهِ تَطِــــــــيبُ

إِذَا ذُكِرَ الْمَحْبُوبُ عِنْدَ حَبِيْـــــبِهِ   تَرَنَّحَ نَشْوَان وَحَنَّ طَـــــــرُوبُ

By the remembrance of Allah, hearts find comfort ...
And our world is made good by His remembrance
When the beloved is mentioned to the lover ...
He sways, intoxicated, and yearns passionately

A FESTIVITY OF OFFERING THANKS & GRATITUDE TO ALMIGHTY ALLAH

In the days of *Tashrīq*, the believers enjoy the pleasure of their bodies through eating and drinking, and the pleasure of their hearts through remembrance and gratitude; thus, the blessing is completed.

Whenever they offer thanks for a blessing, their gratitude itself becomes another blessing, requiring further thanks, and thus, gratitude never ends.

إِذَا كَانَ شُكْرِى نِعْمَةَ اللهِ نِعْمَةً   عَلَيَّ لَهُ فِى مِثْلِهَا يَجِبُ الشُّكْرُ

فَكَيْفَ بُلُوغَ الشُّكْرِ إِلَّا بِفَضْلِهِ   وَإِنْ طَالَتِ الْأَيَّامُ وَاتَّصَلَ الْعُمْرُ

If my gratitude for Allah's blessing is itself a blessing ...
Then I must thank Him for it, which requires further thanks
How can one reach complete gratitude except by His grace ...
Even if the days prolong and life extends

In the saying of the Prophet ﷺ: "*They are days of eating, drinking, and remembrance of Allah the Exalted;*" there is an indication that eating and drinking during the days of 'Īd are meant to help in remembering and obeying Allah.

This is part of complete gratitude for the blessing, as one uses it for obedience.

Allah the Exalted has commanded in His Book to eat from the good things and thank Him [through acts of obedience].

Whoever uses Allah's blessings for disobedience has indeed been ungrateful for Allah's blessing and has exchanged it for ingratitude, and he is deserving of being deprived of it, as it is said:

إِذَا كُنْتَ فِي نِعْمَةٍ فَارْعِهَا   فَإِنَّ الْمَعَاصِى تُزِيلُ النِّعَمْ

وَدَاوِمْ عَلَيْهَا بِشُكْرِ الْإِلهِ   فَشُكْرُ الْإِلهِ يُزِيلُ النِّقَمْ

If you are in a blessing, take care of it ...
For sins remove blessings
And persist in it with gratitude to Allah ...
For gratitude to Allah removes afflictions

WISDOMS OF SLAUGHTERING THE SACRIFICIAL ANIMAL

Especially the blessing of eating from the meat of sacrificial animals, as in the days of *Tashrīq*; for these animals are obedient to Allah and do not disobey Him. They glorify Him and are devoted to Him, as Allah Almighty said:

﴿ وَإِن مِّن شَيْءٍ إِلَّا يُسَبِّحُ بِحَمْدِهِۦ وَلَـٰكِن لَّا تَفْقَهُونَ تَسْبِيحَهُمْ ﴾

And there is not a thing except that it proclaims His purity
supplemented with His praise.
[Al-Isrā' : 44]

And they prostrate to Him, as mentioned in Sūrah An-Naḥl and Sūrah Al-Ḥajj.

They might even remember Allah more than some human beings.

In the '*Musnad*', it is reported:

« رُبَّ بَهِيمَةٍ خَيْرٌ مِن رَاكِبِهَا ، وَأَكْثَرُ لله مِنْهُ ذِكْرًا »

Perhaps an animal is better than its rider
and remembers Allah more than him. [1]

Almighty Allah has informed us in His Book that many among the jinn and humans are like cattle, *"rather even more astray."*

Allah the Exalted permitted the slaughter of these obedient, remembering animals for His believing servants, so that their bodies may be strengthened and their pleasures completed through eating meat, as it is among the finest and most delightful foods.

Although bodies can subsist on plants and other foods, strength, intellect, and pleasure are only perfected with meat.

Therefore, Allah permitted the believers to slaughter these animals and eat their meat, thus enhancing the strength and intellect of His servants, helping them in acquiring beneficial knowledge and performing righteous deeds by which humans are distinguished from animals, and aiding them in the *dhikr* of Almighty Allah, which is more than that of the animals.

Therefore, it is not fitting for a believer to do anything but respond to these blessings with gratitude and use them to obey Allah the Exalted and remember Him, as Allah has favoured the children of Adam over many of His creations and subjected these animals to them.

Allah the Exalted said:

﴿ فَكُلُواْ مِنْهَا وَأَطْعِمُواْ ٱلْقَانِعَ وَٱلْمُعْتَرَّ كَذَلِكَ سَخَّرْنَـٰهَا لَكُمْ لَعَلَّكُمْ تَشْكُرُونَ ﴾

Then eat from them and feed the needy and the beggar. In this way have
We subjugated them for you so that you may be grateful. [Al-Ḥajj : 36]

---

[1] Reported by Aḥmad (441, 440, 3/439.

As for those who slaughter these obedient, remembering animals and then use their meat to disobey Allah the Exalted and forget His remembrance, they have reversed the order and been ungrateful for the blessing.

Such people are worse than and less obedient than the animals.

نَهَارُكَ يَا مَغْرُورُ سَهْوٌ وَغَفْلَةٌ   وَلَيْلُكَ نَوْمٌ والرَّدِىُ لَكَ لَازِمُ

وَتَتْعَبُ فِيْمَا سَوْفَ تَكْرَهُ غِبَّهُ   كَذَلِكَ فِي الدُّنْيَا تَعِيْشُ الْبَهَائِمُ

Your day, O deluded one, is spent in heedlessness and negligence ...
And your night in sleep, while death is inevitable for you
And you toil for what you will regret later ...
Similarly, in this world do animals live

'ĪD AS HOSPITALITY FROM ALMIGHTY ALLAH

The prohibition of fasting on the days of *Tashrīq* is because they are days of 'Īd for Muslims, along with the Day of *Naḥr*. Therefore, fasting is not allowed in Minā or elsewhere according to the majority of scholars; except for 'Aṭā', who said that the prohibition is specific to the people of Minā. The prohibition applies to voluntary fasting, whether it coincides with a regular practice or not.

As for fasting them as compensation for a missed obligatory fast or a vow, or fasting them in Minā for the one performing *tamattu'* who cannot find a sacrificial animal, there is well-known disagreement among scholars.

Most scholars make no distinction between these days; except for Mālik, who said that fasting on the third day is permissible specifically for a vow.

There is a beautiful wisdom in the prohibition of fasting these days and the command to eat and drink during them, which is that Almighty Allah knew the hardships faced by those who journey to His

House, the fatigue of *iḥrām*, and the striving of their souls to complete the rites.

He prescribed for them to rest after that by staying in Minā on the Day of *Naḥr* and the three days following it, and He commanded them to eat from the meat of their sacrifices.

They are in the hospitality of Allah the Exalted during these days as a kindness, compassion, and mercy from Allah.

The people in the [other] lands also participate in this, as they share in the efforts dedicated to Allah and strive during the first ten days of Dhu al-Hijjah through fasting, remembrance, and exertion in worship.

They also share in attaining forgiveness and drawing closer to Allah by offering the sacrificial animals.

Thus, they share in the celebration of 'Īd and all rest during the days of 'Īd by eating and drinking, just as they shared in the effort and dedication during the ten days.

All Muslims are in the hospitality of Allah the Exalted during these days, eating from His provision and thanking Him for His bounty.

Fasting these days was prohibited because it is not fitting for the generous to make his guests hungry.

It is as if it was said to the believers during these days: Your work, which you have done, is complete, and now all that remains for you is rest; this rest is a reward for that effort, just as the fasters for Allah in the month of *Ramaḍān* were commanded to break their fast on the day of *'Īd al-Fiṭr*.

THE RITES: A PARABLE OF THE BELIEVER'S CONDITION

From this, an indication of the believer's condition in this world can be understood; the entire world is like the days of travel, like the days of

Ḥajj, and it is a time of *iḥrām* for the believer from what Allah has forbidden of desires.

Whoever endures during the period of his travel with his *iḥrām* and refrains from desire, when his journey of life ends and he reaches the Minā of his desires, he has completed his purification and fulfilled his vows. His days become like the days of Minā, days of eating, drinking, and remembrance of Allah the Exalted, and he is in the hospitality of Allah the Exalted, in His company forever and ever.

Thus, it is said to the people of Paradise:

﴿ كُلُواْ وَٱشْرَبُواْ هَنِيٓئًا بِمَا كُنتُمْ تَعْمَلُونَ ﴾

Eat and drink wholeheartedly in satisfaction for what you used to do
[Al-Ṭūr : 19]

and

﴿ كُلُواْ وَٱشْرَبُواْ هَنِيٓئًا بِمَآ أَسْلَفْتُمْ فِى ٱلْأَيَّامِ ٱلْخَالِيَةِ ﴾

Eat and drink wholeheartedly in satisfaction for what you did in the days past
[Al-Ḥāqqah : 24]

It has been said that this was revealed concerning those who fasted in this world.

RIGHTEOUS FASTING

وَقَدْ صُمْتُ عَنْ لَذَّاتِ دَهْرِئ كُلّهَا   وَيَوْمَ لِقَاكُمْ ذَاكَ فِطْرُ صِيَامِئ

I have abstained from all the pleasures of my time ...
And the day I meet you will be the breaking of my fast

Some of the pious predecessors said: Fast from the world and make your breaking of the fast at death.

فَصُمْ يَوْمَكَ الْأَدْنَى لَعَلَّكَ فِى غَدٍ   تَفُوزُ بِعِيدِ الْفِطْرِ وَالنَّاسُ صَوَّمُ

Fast from the nearest day so that tomorrow ...
> *You may celebrate ‘Īd al-Fiṭr while others are still fasting*

Whoever fasts today from his desires will break his fast upon them tomorrow after his death.

Whoever hastens to indulge in what is forbidden of his pleasures will be punished by being deprived of his share of Paradise and its loss; evidence of this is that whoever drinks wine in this world will not drink it in the Hereafter, and whoever wears silk will not wear it in the Hereafter.

أَنْتَ فِى دَارِ شَــــتَاتٍ   فَتَــأَهَّبْ لِشَتَــــاتِكَ

وَاجْعَلِ الدُّنْـــيَا كَيَوْمٍ   صُمْتَهُ عَنْ شَهَــــوَاتِكَ

وَلْيَكُنْ فِطْـــركَ عِنْدَ اللّــ   ـهِ فِى يَوْمِ وَفَــــاتِكَ

You are in a house of dispersion ...
> *So prepare for your dispersion*

And make the world like a day ...
> *You have fasted from your desires*

And let your breaking of the fast be with Allah ...
> *On the day of your death*

PARADISE: THE HOSPITALITY OF ALMIGHTY ALLAH

Allah the Exalted said:

﴿ وَٱللَّهُ يَدْعُوٓاْ إِلَىٰ دَارِ ٱلسَّلَـٰمِ وَيَهْدِى مَن يَشَآءُ إِلَىٰ صِرَاطٍ مُّسْتَقِيمٍ ﴾

And Allah invites to the Abode of Peace and
He guides whom He wills to the straight path
[Yūnus : 25]

Paradise is the hospitality of Allah, prepared as a dwelling for His believing servants, containing what no eye has seen, no ear has heard, and no human heart has ever conceived.

The Messenger of Allah ﷺ was sent to call people to it through faith, Islam, and excellence.

Whoever responds will enter Paradise and partake in that hospitality, and whoever does not respond will be deprived of it.

Tirmidhī recorded from Jābir ﷺ, who said: One day the Messenger of Allah ﷺ came out to us and said:

«رَأَيْتُ فِي المَنَامِ كَأَنَّ جِبْرِيلَ عِنْدَ رَأْسِي وَمِيكَائِيلَ عِنْدَ رِجْلِيّ ، فَقَالَ أَحَدُهُمَا لِصَاحِبِهِ : اضرِبْ لَهُ مَثَلًا ، فَقَالَ : اسمَع سَمِعَتْ أُذْنُكَ ، وَاعْقِلْ عَقَلَ قَلْبُكَ ؛ إِنَّمَا مَثَلُكَ وَمَثَلُ أُمَّتِكَ كَمَثَلِ مَلِكٍ اتَّخَذَ دَارًا ، ثُمَّ بَنَى فِيهَا بَيْتًا ، وَجَعَلَ فِيهَا مَائِدَةً ، ثُمَّ بَعَثَ رَسُولًا يَدْعُو النَّاسَ إِلَى طَعَامِهِ ؛ فَمِنْهُمْ مَنْ أَجَابَ الرَّسُولَ ، وَمِنْهُمْ مَنْ تَرَكَهُ ، فَاللهُ تَعَالَى : هُوَ المَلِكُ ، وَالدَّارُ هِيَ الإِسْلَامُ ، وَالبَيْتُ الجَنَّةُ ، وَأَنْتَ يَا مُحَمَّدُ رَسُولٌ ، مَنْ أَجَابَكَ دَخَلَ الإِسْلَامَ ، وَمَنْ دَخَلَ الإِسْلَامَ دَخَلَ الجَنَّةَ ، وَمَنْ دَخَلَ الجَنَّةَ أَكَلَ مَا فِيهَا »

I saw in my dream that Jibrā'īl was at my head and Mīkā'īl at my feet. One of them said to the other: "Set forth a parable for him." The other said: "Listen with your ear and understand with your heart! Your example and the example of your nation is like that of a king who built a dwelling, then made a feast therein and sent a messenger to invite the people to his food. Some responded to the messenger, and some did not. Allah is the King, the dwelling is Islam, the house is Paradise, and you, O Muhammad, are the Messenger. Whoever responds to you enters Islam, and whoever enters Islam enters Paradise, and whoever enters Paradise eats from its contents." [1]

Bukhārī recorded it with a similar meaning, and its wording is: *"His example is like that of a man who built a house, made a feast therein, and*

---

[1] Reported by Tirmidhī (2860), who said: This ḥadīth has been narrated through other chains from the Prophet ﷺ with a more authentic *isnād*, and it is a *mursal ḥadīth*. It is also mentioned by Bukhārī (7281).

sent a caller. Whoever responds to the caller enters the house and eats from the feast, and whoever does not respond to the caller does not enter the house and does not eat from the feast; the house is Paradise, and the caller is Muhammad .” [1]

OUR FESTIVALS: ANSWERING THE CALL OF ALLAH

In some Israelite traditions, Almighty Allah: “*O son of Adam, you have not been fair to Me. I remember you, but you forget Me. I call you to Me, but you flee from Me to others. I remove calamities from you, while you remain attached to sins. O son of Adam, what will be your excuse tomorrow when you come to Me?*”

Blessed is the one who responds to his Lord,

﴿ يٰقَوْمَنَآ أَجِيْبُوْا دَاعِىَ اللهِ ﴾

O our people, respond to the Caller of Allah
[Al-Aḥqāf : 31]

يَا نَفْسُ وَيْحَكِ قَدْ أَتَاكِ هُدَاكِ   أَجِيْبِيْ فَدَاعِى الْحَقِّ قَدْ نَادَاكِ

كَمْ قَدْ دُعِيتِ إِلَى الرَّشَادِ فتعرضى   وَأَجِبْتِ دَاعِىَ الْغَيِّ حِيْنَ دَعَاكِ

O soul, woe to you, your guidance has come ...
Answer, for the Caller of truth has called you
How many times have you been called to guidance but turned away ...
And you answered the call of misguidance when it called you

Everything in this world reminds us of the Hereafter; its seasons, festivals, and joys remind us of the seasons, festivals, and joys of the Hereafter.

---

[1] Reported by Bukhārī (7281).

'Abd al-Wāḥid ibn Zayd prepared food for his brothers, and 'Utbah al-Ghulām stood serving them while fasting. 'Abd al-Wāḥid kept watching him, stealing glances, and saw 'Utbah's tears flowing.

Later, he asked him about his crying at that time, and he said: "I remembered the tables of Paradise and the young boys standing around them," and 'Abd al-Wāḥid fell unconscious.

The bodies of the knowers are in this world, but their hearts are in the Hereafter.

جِسْمِي مَعِي غَيْرَ أَنَّ الرُّوحَ عِنْدَكُمُ   فَالْجِسْمُ فِي غُرْبَةٍ وَّالرُّوحُ فِي وَطَنِ

My body is with me, but my soul is with you ...
The body is in exile, but the soul is in its homeland

STAYING AWAY FROM DISOBEDIENCE: THE ULTIMATE FESTIVAL

The festivals of people come to an end, but the festivals of the knowers are continuous.

Al-Ḥasan said: Every day you do not disobey Allah is a day of celebration for you!

Someone came to one of the knowers of Allah, greeted him, and said: "I want to speak with you." He replied: "Today is a festival for us." So, the man left him.

He came another day and said the same thing, and again he replied: "Today is a festival for us."

He came yet another day and received the same response. The man said: "How many festivals do you have?"

He replied: "O idle one! Don't you know that every day we do not disobey Allah is a festival for us?!"

The times of the knowers are all joy and happiness in their communion with their Lord and His remembrance, thus they are festivals.

Al-Shibli used to recite:

فَمَا أَضْنَعُ بِالْعِـــــيدِ   إِذَا مَا كُنْتَ لِي عِـــــيْدًا

كَجَرْيِ الْمَـــــاءِ فِي الْعُودِ   جَـــرَى حُبُّكَ فِي قَلْبِي

If you are my festival ...

> *What need do I have for a festival*

Your love flows in my heart ...

> *Like water flows through a stick*

It was also recited:

وَالْقَلْبُ مِنِّي عَنِ اللَّذَّاتِ مُنْحَرِفُ   عِيدِى مُقِيْمٌ وَعِيدُ النَّاسِ مُنْصَرِفُ

طُول الْحَنِين وَعَيْن دَمْعِهَا يَكف   وَلِيْ قَرِينَانِ مَا لِي مِنْهُمَا خَلَفُ

My festival is constant and people's festivals pass ...

> *And my heart is turned away from pleasures*

I have two companions who never leave me ...

> *Longing and eyes that shed tears*

لَا إِلَهَ إِلَّا اللهُ وَحْدَهُ
لَا شَرِيكَ لَهُ
لَهُ الْمُلْكُ وَلَهُ الْحَمْدُ
وَهُوَ عَلَى كُلِّ شَيْءٍ قَدِيرٌ.